SENTRY HILL

AN ULSTER FARM AND FAMILY

SENTRY HILL

AN ULSTER FARM AND FAMILY

BRIAN M. WALKER

Brian M. Walker

BLACKSTAFF PRESS

Frontispiece:

William McKinney in the
conservatory at Sentry Hill, *c.*1905.

Cover illustrations

Front cover: 'Sentry Hill' by J.W. Carey, from a
hand-illustrated album presented to W.F. McKinney in
1905.
Back cover: Some members of the McKinney family at
Sentry Hill, 1905 (W.McK.).
Front: Jack and Bessie Dundee.
Seated: Meg and Hugh McKinney.
Standing: Elsie, Lorra (Hugh's daughter) and Tom
McKinney.

British Library Cataloguing in Publication Data

Walker, Brian Mercer
    Sentry Hill
    1. Farm life – Northern Ireland – Carnmoney
    region – History
    2. Sentry Hill
    I. Title
    941.6'18   DA990.A6

    ISBN 0–85640–254–0

Published by Blackstaff Press Limited
3 Galway Park, Dundonald, BT16 0AN

Printed in Northern Ireland by Nicholson & Bass Limited

Dedicated to
Dr Joe McKinney Dundee
who has wrought hard
in the fields of his forefathers

Meg McKinney on the front lawn
of Sentry Hill, *c.*1907 (W.McK.).
To the left are John and Samuel
McKinney.

A Prayer

Not for the good of your souls but my book.

———

You who for reading feel a boundless rage,
And penetrate beyond the title page,
To you this rude petition I address,
In hopes you'll kindly lessen my distress.
But chiefly, Ladies, your support I crave,
O, deign your helpless supplicant to save!
In me you view a wretch of strength devoid,
Like you, too often neglected when enjoyed.
Ah! make me then the object of your care,
Tear not my leaves to ornament your hair.
If married, save me from your children's gripe,
Nor let my pages light your husband's pipe.
If I attend you when you sip your tea,
Be careful not to spill it over me.
Fill not my bosom when you eat, with crumbs;
Turn me not over with damp or greasy thumbs.
Aside your face turn when you sneeze or cough;
And spare my corners when you last leave off.
Avert such ills! or I, exposed to all,
May, unoffending, prematurely fall.
So shall my pages legible remain,
And at some future period ease your pain:
Amusement with instruction thrive to blend,
And soothe your sorrows when you want a friend.
So may your days be spent in social peace,
Your cares diminish and your joys increase;
Your charms shine forth unrivall'd to the view,
And gain the homage to your merit due.

Unpublished poem by Samuel Walker
of
Shane's Hill, near Templepatrick

Abbreviations of photographers' names used in captions

D.D.	Dermott Dunbar
H.	Hale (a Belfast photographer of 1870)
H.C.	Herbert Carlisle
J.McK.D	Joe McKinney Dundee
R.W.	Robert Welch
W. McK.	William Fee McKinney

Contents

Preface

In 1976 I was invited by Conor O'Clery of *The Irish Times* to look at a collection of old photographs which had recently been brought to his attention. The visit to Whitehead, in Co. Antrim, which followed revealed a number of fascinating photographs of country life at the turn of the century. More importantly, however, this trip resulted in another visit, this time to the family home of the owner of the collection, at Sentry Hill, Carnmoney. The impression which this second visit created is still vivid in my mind. Sentry Hill looks like a fairly typical nineteenth-century Antrim farmhouse and the name of the McKinney family meant nothing to me. But that outing on a Sunday afternoon in September 1976 was to open the door on to the home and life of a very remarkable family.

The McKinneys were ordinary people in most ways. They were prosperous farmers who played a full if unspectacular part in their rural community. What *was* special about them, however, was that they accumulated and preserved an amazing amount of material about their lives and those of the people around them. This was particularly true of one member of the family: William Fee McKinney (1832–1917). He wrote diaries, which was unusual enough for a nineteenth-century farmer, and he held on to all the papers and records of the various local organisations to which he belonged, such as the reading club, the temperance society, his dispensary and church committees. He retained an enormous variety of the ephemera of everyday life, from tram-tickets to receipts. In addition, he built up an extensive photographic record of life on his farm and in the neighbourhood, something which very few contemporary photographers bothered with.

All these papers and photographs were still at Sentry Hill. I remember clearly opening a drawer in a bureau and finding some telegrams and letters from the War Office, dated 1916. They informed the family that young Tom McKinney had been wounded at the Somme, then that he had died, and finally listed his belongings which had been dispatched home. It seemed as if these papers had been placed there only a few days before. But more than this, the fabric and belongings of the farm had remained virtually untouched since the early decades of the century. Furniture, glass, books, and other items collected in the nineteenth century were to be found all around the house; some even had labels from eighty years ago saying how the family had come to possess them. The house itself had altered little since the First World War.

This material at Sentry Hill, both documents and objects, was only part

This photograph of Sentry Hill was taken by Robert Welch in 1893. Four generations of McKinneys were present for the occasion, including Thomas George McKinney (1807–1893), his son William (1832–1917), his grandson John (1862–1934), and his great grand-daughter Elsie who was still alive when I visited Sentry Hill in 1976.

of the picture which emerged at that original visit. Although I had already met the owner, Dr Joe Dundee, grandson of William McKinney, at Whitehead, it was not until our meeting at Sentry Hill that it became apparent that here was a very unusual individual who effectively complemented the material at his family home. Now a retired country doctor, Joe has always been an acute observer of country life. It is entirely due to his efforts that Sentry Hill and its treasures have survived. His willing guidance and his perception have helped me to make sense of all this material and to describe the world it records.

This world began as a strange, hidden one for me. These people were farmers, Presbyterians and descendants of Scots. Nothing of my own background fell into these categories, so it meant exploring totally new areas. It involved learning about farming, and seeing the land from the viewpoint of the people who 'wrought hard' to make a living from it and who have left their mark on the landscape. The countryside today bears witness to the efforts of their labours. Other aspects of their lives, however, have been completely submerged by the modern world.

The advance of this modern world can be seen only too clearly in the present position of Sentry Hill. It now lies close to a motorway and not far from the sprawling conglomeration of Newtownabbey which has already engulfed most of the parish. Urban, industrialised society is now what most of us can expect for the future, but it is not so long ago that our forebears were based on the land. And here the McKinney material allows us an invaluable glimpse of a lost age. The McKinneys are a special family in some ways, but in others they are quite typical, and so their story provides an insight into the working lives and social activities of ordinary rural families, the sort of people about whom the records are usually fairly scanty.

Besides such information, the material at Sentry Hill gives a fascinating view of people's attitudes and values, and how these have changed, especially among the Presbyterian community. It was surprising to discover, for example, that in the early nineteenth century Presbyterians were very tolerant towards alcohol and its consumption. The experiences of the McKinneys illustrate well some of the important changes in religious and cultural as well as political matters which have occurred in our society over the last two hundred years.

I hope that the reader will find something of worth in this book. Certainly, for myself the writing of it has been an invaluable experience. Its value, however, lies only partly in what I have learnt. It lies also in the pleasure of having known Joe Dundee over this period of research and writing. His hospitality and advice, as well as that of his sister, Mrs Isobel Crozier, have made the writing of this book a very pleasant and rewarding experience, for which I am deeply grateful.

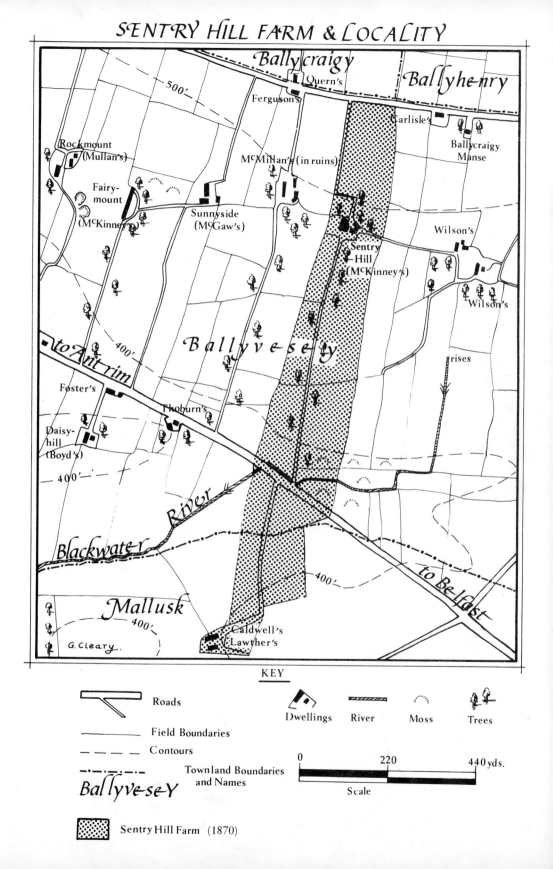

SENTRY HILL FARM & LOCALITY

Ballycraigy
Quern's
Ferguson's
Ballyhenry
Carlisle's
Ballycraigy Manse
Rockmount (Mullan's)
McMillan's (in ruins)
Fairy-mount (McKinney's)
Sunnyside (McGaw's)
Sentry Hill (McKinney's)
Wilson's
Wilson's
Ballyvesely
rises
Foster's
Thoburn's
to Antrim
Daisy-hill (Boyd's)
River
Blackwater
Mallusk
to Belfast
Caldwell's
Lawther's
G. Cleary.

500'
400'
400'
400'
400'

KEY

| | Roads | | Dwellings | River | Moss | Trees |

Field Boundaries

Contours

Ballyvesey — Townland Boundaries and Names

Scale 0 — 220 — 440 yds.

Sentry Hill Farm (1870)

1
Early Days
Sentry Hill from early times to 1832

In the early summer of 1689 supporters of William of Orange dispatched a sentry to a hill-top five miles south of Carrickfergus. His mission was to keep a look-out for the movements of Jacobite troops in the area. From that time on, the hill has been known as 'Sentry Hill'. Today there are several farmhouses on its slopes, including one which also bears the name Sentry Hill. This is the home of the McKinney family who first settled there in the late eighteenth century. Ironically it was because of their Jacobite sympathies that they had left Scotland earlier in that century. It is this farm and family which first seized my interest on that afternoon in September 1976 and which is the centre of our story.

The view from the top of Sentry Hill takes in not only Carrickfergus but also much of the surrounding countryside. The hill is in fact part of a ridge which runs eastward from Lough Neagh, past Carnmoney village, to Carnmoney Hill. To the south and directly in front of the house stand Cavehill, Colinward, Squire's Hill, the Bohill, and Lyle Hill, with Glengormley, Hydepark, and Mallusk in the valley between. To the north another valley, containing the river known as the Three-Mile-Water and industrial areas such as Mossley and Monkstown, rises steeply to the Knockagh Hill; in the distance Slemish can be seen.

The sight to the east from Carnmoney was described by Thomas Houston, a friend of William McKinney's, in 1893:

From The Book of the Grand Bazaar and Fancy Fair at Carnmoney (Belfast, 1893), pp.21–2.

On a clear day the view from Carnmoney Hill is exceedingly fine, ranging from Scotland to the Mourne Mountains; while near at hand, spread out like a great green carpet, is the flat meadow land between Belfast and Carrickfergus, and noble mansions, clumps of trees, a village factory and church are but like furniture . . . And there, too, is the railway track, and upon it is the iron horse; but up so high as we are now the train seems only like a toy for children. And beyond is Belfast Lough, with placid waters.

Most of this 'great green carpet' has now of course been built up.

The first members of the McKinney family, James and Helen, arrived in the area from Scotland in 1716. James was a Highlander who had fought on the side of the Stuarts in the rising of 1715 and after their defeat at the battle of Sheriffmuir he had felt it expedient to leave his native Rosshire. Beside the political, there were strong personal reasons for his departure. Helen's clan, the Campbells, had fought for the Hanoverian side and were totally opposed to any marriage with a 'rebel'. James and Helen therefore decided to forsake Scotland and go to Ireland. They married and settled in Carnmoney, although it was not until the 1780s that a grandson, Andrew,

The slopes of Carnmoney Hill, c.1900, taken by William McKinney. The figures in the foreground are all members of the Dawson family of Cloughfern.

1

Aerial view of Sentry Hill, 1981
(Skyviews and General Ltd).

occupied Sentry Hill. Now, two centuries and seven generations on, Sentry Hill is still in the family, in the person of Dr Joe Dundee, whose mother was a McKinney.

The house today is an attractive, late-Victorian dwelling, with horizontally-divided sash windows and a small conservatory over the front porch. It was built originally in 1835 to replace a two-storeyed thatched cottage, and extensively renovated and altered fifty years later. Only a few windows with Georgian glazing bars at one side of the house date back to 1835. The construction of a bathroom and an extra bedroom over the kitchen in the 1920s and a porch at the back door in 1981 have not affected the essentially Victorian character and charm of the house.

Sentry Hill sits about half-way up the hillside. A broad lawn slopes down from the front of the house and is bordered by attractive beds of flowers and shrubs, giving it a pleasant, open setting. The front and back drives are flanked by large beech trees, planted in the 1830s by Thomas George McKinney. The front drive, which formerly ran straight down to the main Antrim road, can no longer be used because the new motorway has cut across it. The entrance to the house today is once again via the old Irish Highway (originally the main route from Carrickfergus to Antrim), then down a twisting back drive to the farm buildings.

For this reason, the visitor now enters the house by the kitchen, a warm friendly place, with scrubbed pine furniture and an old-fashioned range. A high shelf displays some of the family's pewterware now no longer in daily use. From the kitchen the remains of the original flagged hallway into the rest of the house can be seen. Stepping into this hall, one walks through the door which was once the back entrance to the 1835 house and which still retains the massive iron bar used to reinforce it against intruders.

The layout of the interior has altered little since the renovations of the 1880s. The dining-room has been extended to include what was formerly a small store-room. Near the fireplace what looks like a cupboard door is in fact the disguised entrance to a tiny bathroom, said to be one of the first built in an Irish farmhouse. The original Victorian fittings are still there, complete with brass taps and ornamentation, including a small lion's head in the centre of the washbasin.

The furniture and belongings, accumulated over many generations, give the place a special atmosphere. The Chippendale chairs in the dining-room were obtained in the late 1830s from an earlier McKinney home at the Burnt Hill, Carnmoney. Victorian bureaux and display cabinets contain pieces of eighteenth- and nineteenth-century glass, pottery, pewter, and brassware. A few of these objects commemorate events such as the Fall of the Bastille and Queen Victoria's Diamond Jubilee but most are the ordinary, everyday things of the McKinney family which have somehow survived. No substantial nineteenth-century farmhouse would be complete, of course, without a grandfather clock and at Sentry Hill there are no fewer than three.

In the attic, however, the scene is rather less typical. William McKinney

View of the dining room at Sentry Hill, 1980 (D.D.). Two of the Chippendale chairs which came from the Burnt Hill home of the McKinneys can be seen.

was an avid collector, not only of local archaeological finds but of an amazing range of bits and pieces, and his collection is now laid out in one of the attic rooms. Cases of flints and fossils, and displays of curios sent back from the colonies are placed side by side with old kitchen implements. Spears and pikes from the '98 rebellion decorate the walls; a bundle of walking sticks, one belonging to a long-dead African chief, stand beside the door. A splash of flamboyance is given by the case of birds of paradise at the window.

The other attic room, with its bookshelves, boxes and trunks, is less immediately interesting. But it is here that we find the real treasures of Sentry Hill, the things which make it unique. These boxes are full of papers, cuttings, battered old account books, receipts – all the paperwork of a nineteenth-century Presbyterian farmer who took a lively interest in all that went on around him. Cupboards and chests in the bedrooms reveal albums of family photographs and boxes of glass negatives, for William McKinney was also an extraordinarily keen photographer. Over six hundred photographs, taken between 1890 and 1917, still survive at Sentry Hill. It is these papers and photographs which reveal the story of Sentry Hill and of the McKinney family.

When the McKinneys acquired Sentry Hill in the 1780s, they were, of course, only the latest in a long succession of people who had settled and worked in the locality. There is plentiful evidence of the activities of these earlier occupants, as William McKinney recorded in some notes on the history of Carnmoney in the 1880s:

> The principal instruments that I have seen that were found in this neighbourhood are stone and bronze celts, flint arrowheads, and bronze and iron spear heads, from which I am led to conclude that our forefathers in Carnmoney had a decided taste for offensive and defensive warfare. Some of the weapons that I have seen are evidently very well adapted for 'letting out lives'.

At Sentry Hill, McKinney built up a good collection of stone chisel-edged implements, or 'celts', as he called them. They include some flints of mesolithic man, the first people to settle in Ireland, and stone axes belonging to the second wave of settlers in the neolithic period. These were picked up in the surrounding fields, not only by William McKinney but also, later, by his grandson, Joe, the present owner of the farm. Cairns, or the remains of cairns, are further evidence of neolithic man in the area and are to be seen on most of the neighbouring hills: Squire's Hill, Colinward, the Bohill. The name Carnmoney actually means 'the cairn in the shrubbery' – though locals, thinking that the name suggested the presence of money or treasure, dug up part of Carnmoney Hill in the early nineteenth century!

The bronze implements mentioned by William belong to the next period, the bronze age, but there are none in his collection: an observer in the 1830s stated that farmers were then in the habit of selling them to tinkers. Behind the outbuildings at Sentry Hill there is a standing stone

The hallway at Sentry Hill, looking from the kitchen towards the front lawn, 1980 (D.D.).

5

from this period. It links with another stone at nearby Fairymount to mark a route between the Carnmoney and Lyle hills; the latter was an important enclosure and habitation site in the late bronze age.

There are many examples of raths and souterrains from the early Christian period. At Carnmoney and Monkstown there were churches, dating probably from the seventh century, but nothing now remains of them. The stream which flows past the present day Carnmoney parish church, the site of the original church (called Coole), was known for many centuries as Glas-na-Braddon. One translation of this is 'Little Brigid's River' and it is possible the church may have been dedicated to St Brigid.

The arrival of the Anglo-Normans in Ulster in the 1170s brought important changes to the landscape. The most obvious evidence of their presence is, of course, Carrickfergus Castle. At the same time a Norman borough was established at Coole, known as Le Coule. Some parts of the district around Sentry Hill were taken over by the Anglo-Normans while others were left to their original inhabitants, as may be deduced from local place-names. Ballyvesey, the townland in which Sentry Hill stands, was probably called after some Anglo-Norman family: the prefix Bally- comes from the Irish *baile*, meaning, roughly, 'town' or 'townland'. Who Vesey was is not clear, although it is likely that he was a Norman knight.

John McKinney on a side car in the front avenue, *c*.1905, with his sister Meg (*right*) and a family friend, Mary Bird (W.McK.).

Neighbouring Mallusk became an Anglo-Norman grange, that is, farm-land managed by a monastic house under the influence of the Normans. This explains why the townland is known as the Grange of Mallusk. Most of the other townland names in the area are also from the Irish and refer to either Irish families or to the geographical setting: Glengormley means 'glen of the Princess Gormlaith (daughter of a ninth-century Ulster king)'; Ballycraigy, 'the townland of the rocks'.

By the end of the fourteenth century the O'Neills of Tyrone had established their authority over the region and set up a separate kingdom of which Sentry Hill was now a part. In the course of the sixteenth century the O'Neills were challenged by the central English authorities in Dublin and by the end of the century Sir Arthur Chichester had firmly established the power of the Crown in East Antrim. Coole was completely destroyed during the wars of this period. Antrim was not part of the Ulster plantation but in the early 1600s the land was divided and granted to various people, some of whom had held their land for some time, and others more recently arrived. Chichester, whose descendants later assumed the title of Donegall, acquired very substantial lands in South and East Antrim, including Sentry Hill and all of Carnmoney parish. From early in the seventeenth century, immigrants, especially from Scotland, settled on Chichester's land. In spite of the arrival of these new inhabitants, there were still former Irish inhabitants in the area. A description of a Lt Barry's house in 1611 at Whiteabbey remarked that near the house were 'many

Quoted in H.J. St J. Clarke, *Thirty Centuries in S.E. Antrim* (Belfast, 1938), p.123.

other tenemtes inhabited, some of them by such cyvell Irish as doe speake English, and dyvers of them have bynne servitors in the late Queen's tyme'.

In 1641 a rebellion broke out which affected this region as well as the rest of the country. Started by some of the older Irish families as a war against the Crown it soon became a religious civil war. Massacres of Protestants, both English and Scottish, led to retaliation against Catholics, as indicated in two incidents in our district. Writing in *The Ulster Journal of Archaeology* in 1855, a member of the McKinney family described how Burnt Hill in Carnmoney had received its name. In 1641 Catholics attacked and burned the home of a Protestant family called Johnston who lived on this hill. All the inmates were put to death except one son, who escaped and was sheltered by a Catholic family near Whitehouse. According to editorial comment in the journal, this tradition was handed down to McKinney by an old woman of eighty-seven years of age who lived at the McKinneys' home on the Burnt Hill. On the other side, reacting

See Clarke, *op. cit.*, p.144.

to reports of the massacre of their families in Tyrone, a troop of soldiers are supposed to have marched from Antrim to Templepatrick and murdered Catholic families in revenge.

The rebellion was eventually put down and new Scottish immigrants, mostly Presbyterian, continued to arrive in the area. Looking at the names in the hearth money returns of the district for 1669 we can see that only a very few were now Irish while the rest were nearly all Scottish Lowlanders. An interesting point about these Scots arises from the 1659 census of

The three Guthrie brothers, King's Moss, *c.*1895 (W.McK.). They are, *from left to right*, James (1822–1901), John (1820–1902) and Sam (1815–1901). The family, who were distant relatives of the McKinneys, had come over from Stirling in Scotland soon after the Revolution of 1689.

Ireland. For this area it divides the population into English and Irish, with no mention of Scots. As has been noted, the names on the 1669 hearth money returns indicated few Irish and, indeed, few English families. The reason for this apparent clash of evidence is found in a footnote which lists the principal Irish names and includes many that are obviously Scottish such as Martin. It seems that the census in fact divides people according to language and includes Scottish families as Irish, probably because they had a knowledge of Gaelic.

A French traveller, de Rochefort, who visited South and East Antrim in the 1660s, described some of the prevailing dietary habits:

> They eat here, as well as in some parts of Scotland, cakes called kets, which they
> bake on thin iron plates over a fire; being sufficiently baked on one side, they

Quoted in Clarke, *op. cit.,* pp.125–6.

turn them on the other, till they become as dry as a biscuit. They are made without leaven and are sometimes so ill baked that a person who is not used to them cannot eat them; nevertheless throughout all the inns on the road no other sort of bread is eaten; however, they do not spare to cover them with butter, and thick cheese, here very cheap, costing only a penny per pound. The common people live chiefly on this, especially in places distant from the rivers and lakes.

The fighting of 1688–90 had little direct effect in the area. During this time, however, local inhabitants did not stay on their farms at night but gathered together in special places which they fortified. One such place was situated at the south-west corner of the townland of Mallusk, at the fort of Ballyvesey and acquired the name of 'The Trench' by which it was afterwards known. After the Battle of the Boyne more immigrants arrived, again mainly from the Lowlands of Scotland. One exception to this general trend occurred in 1716 when the first members of the family at the centre of our story made their appearance.

In 1716 James McKenzie left Scotland for Ireland with his bride-to-be Helen Campbell. Both were Highlanders. According to William McKinney, James's father had lived for a time on the Stewart lands at Killymoon in Co. Tyrone but then returned to Scotland. In spite of this apparent connection with mid Ulster, however, James and Helen decided to settle in Co. Antrim. According to family tradition, in their haste to leave Scotland, all they brought with them was a sword and a cooking-pot. Certainly we know little else about the family in this first half of the eighteenth century. On 5 March 1717 James and Helen were married in Carnmoney Presbyterian meeting house. Two sons were born, John in 1719 and Andrew in 1722. By 1749 the two sons are recorded as being joint tenants on a farm in Carnmoney townland – obviously the Burnt Hill farm which James McKinney, grandson of James McKenzie, occupied in the late eighteenth century.

It is not clear when Helen McKenzie died, although we do know that her husband lived until 1738. By this time the family name, like many others in the neighbourhood, had changed, probably due to the influence of local pronunciation. According to the registers of marriages and baptisms in the Carnmoney Presbyterian session books, James spelt his name *McKenzie* at his marriage in 1717 and again at the baptism of his children. In an address to the Rev. John Thompson in May 1730, however, he signed it *McKinnie*, and his sons' and grandsons' names were spelt in this way until 1791, when his grand-daughter married William Fee; her name was then written *McKinney* and it is this name which is found in subsequent land deeds.

For the first half of the eighteenth century we know that the McKinneys were sub-tenants of middlemen who rented the lands from the Donegall family. None of the McKinneys' land deeds have survived from this period but they probably held their land on similar conditions to James Russell of Ballycraigy, for whom a tenancy indenture, dated 1749, does exist. Russell was obliged to pay his rent half-yearly (approximately five shillings per acre for 22 Irish acres), and to keep houses, ditches, and enclosures in good repair. He was required to grind his corn and grain at the Carnmoney mill or pay a fine. The houses these people lived in were undoubtedly simple thatched cottages.

A rent roll for 1750 for the Carnmoney area has survived and is a valuable record of the occupants at the middle of the century. The names show that most were Lowland Scots. Compared with the list of inhabitants in the 1660s it is interesting how few families go back to the earlier period. W.F. McKinney, who became an expert in local family histories, estimated that in the 1880s more than three-quarters of the farming class in Carnmoney were descended from people who came to the parish *after* the Siege of Derry and not from seventeenth-century settlers.

While documentary evidence of life in this period in Carnmoney is scanty for the most part, fortunately we have an invaluable insight into the religious and social activity of the Presbyterian community through four session books of the Carnmoney Presbyterian church, covering the period 1686–1821. These books, collected and preserved by William McKinney, are amongst the best surviving records of their type. They give the dates of baptisms and marriages, and accounts of the meetings of session (the local governing body of the Presbyterian congregation, composed of the elders). The kirk sessions were concerned not only with spiritual affairs but with enforcing the moral discipline of the congregation, and they played an important part in the social and moral state of the community.

A study of the books reveals the chief concerns of the elders. In February 1697 the session urged that each elder 'duily inform himself within his prospective bounds whether there be any neglect of family worship, or any other scandalous sin and report the same to the session'. At their meetings subjects discussed included the distribution of money to the poor and concern over the low numbers of baptisms. Censure was passed on individuals who worked or used profane language on the sabbath. Alleged cases of witchcraft were investigated by the minister and some elders on a number of occasions.

There were several cases in the early eighteenth century of the session making efforts to reconcile estranged couples. For example, Samuel Thoburn and his wife, Janet Girvan, were reported in 1703 as living apart, but under criticism and advice from some elders they agreed to live together again. 'Scolding wives' and slander were other subjects dealt with. The most important business, however, was sexual morality. Frequently cases of fornication (and occasionally instances of adultery) were discussed at the session. Guilty parties were expected to appear and confess their guilt.

From the middle of the eighteenth century onwards we have more information about the McKinneys and Sentry Hill. James McKenzie's elder son John married one Jennie Evans. Eight children were born of this marriage but by the early nineteenth century, all seem to have died or moved away. Andrew, the second son of James, married Jane Carson in 1750 when she was twenty years old and he twenty-eight. Their eldest son James appears to have held the Burnt Hill farm jointly with his father until

For both the Russell indenture and the rent roll see Clarke, *op. cit.*, pp.174–5.

Drawing by W.W. Houston of Carnmoney parish church before alterations in the nineteenth century

Andrew's death in 1792; James died in 1808 leaving the lease of the farm to his son William who died in 1834 without any children; Burnt Hill was then sold. James's younger brother, John, presumably lived at home until sometime in the 1780s when he became tenant of the Sentry Hill farm.

In a note on the family, William McKinney records that Andrew McKinnie bought Sentry Hill from Robin Robinson for £10. As the Donegalls still owned all the land, what he actually bought was the tenant right and occupancy of the land. John McKinnie is shown in the 1790 tithe records as occupying land in Ballyvesey and the 1802 indenture for Sentry Hill says that he had formerly held this land. The Robinsons had occupied the Sentry Hill farm back into the seventeenth century; their name appears on the Ballyvesey hearth rolls in 1669. William McKinney's wife was descended from the Robinsons; the McKinney family therefore had attachments to Sentry Hill going back to at least the 1660s.

In 1804, at the age of fifty, John married Eliza George, of Welsh descent, from Killead in Co. Antrim. Their first child was born in 1807 and named Thomas George, no doubt after Eliza's father. Eight years later a daughter, Isabella, followed, but she died in infancy. After John's death in 1826, his wife survived him for only another year. Thus at the age of nineteen, Thomas George McKinney became master of Sentry Hill. Five years later he married Isabella Fulton Giffin of neighbouring Ballyduff and they set up home at Sentry Hill.

The latter part of the eighteenth century and the early nineteenth century were times of important development in land-holding in the area. When some of the leases expired in the 1760s and 1770s, rents were raised and new tenants introduced. The unrest which this created led to the growth of a secret agrarian society, the 'Hearts of Steel'. Members burned the homes and haystacks of new tenants. According to William McKinney, an ancestor, William Giffin, had the misfortune to be arrested, on the testimony of an informer who accused him of maliciously setting fire to a

The Boghouse, Ballywonard, c.1895. Formerly the family home of the Giffins, it was occupied at the end of the nineteenth century by the Archbolds, some of whom are seen here with William McKinney. One of William's daughters was married to an Archbold.

haystack, and he was kept in Carrickfergus prison for three months before the trial. The judge dismissed as totally false the evidence of the informer who was duly convicted of perjury, had his ears cropped, and was transported to Botany Bay. Giffin was cleared but his health had suffered during imprisonment and he died from jail fever (typhus), shortly after his release in April 1776.

These agrarian troubles had largely died down by the 1780s and subsequent changes in the Donegall fortunes were to benefit the McKinneys. In an effort to raise money in the 1790s the Donegall family renewed leases on very generous terms in return for immediate cash. Sentry Hill was part of 222 Irish acres in Ballyvesey leased by one James McVicker in 1796. By agreement with McVicker in 1802, John McKinney acquired a 31-year lease on his 20 Irish acres at Sentry Hill. Then in 1826, no doubt because the Donegalls needed more cash and had come to an arrangement with the middleman, John's son Thomas was able to purchase a perpetuity lease which gave him security in return for certain minor obligations. The McKinneys now had almost complete control over Sentry Hill. Two years later Thomas became tenant of another 6 Irish acres adjacent to their land, at Mallusk.

The main commercial centres for the McKinneys at this time were at Parkgate (near Doagh) and Roughfort, where there were important fairs for the sale of livestock and farm produce, though there were smaller fairs at Carnmoney. Amongst William McKinney's papers is a dialect poem by Samuel Thompson (who lived at Lyle Hill, less than a mile from Sentry Hill), describing one such fair in 1790:

> Here grey-clad farmers, gash an' grave
>   Drive in their sleekit hawkeys;
> With monie a slee, auld-farrand knave,
>   To sell their heftit brockeys;
> An' jockey louns, sae gleg an' gare
>   Wi' boot be-deckit legs,
> To glow'r an' drink, cheat, lie an' swear
>   An sell their glossy raigs
>   Come here this day
>
> Here countra' chiels, dock'd aff compleat,
>   Weel sheath'd in Sunday claes,
> Sae trimly as they pace the street,
>   In shoen as black as slaes;
> The lasses fain, come stringing in
>   Frae a' parts o' the country,
> Ilk ane as feat's a new made prin –
>   Ye'd tak them a' for gentry,
>   Sae fine this day
>
> Here chapmen chiels unlock their packs,
>   An' roun' display their toys;
> Intent an' keen to wile the placks
>   Frae silly jades an' boys;
> Ah! bonie young things have a care!
>   Nor let their coaxin' trash
> E'er claim your notice i' the fair,
>   Or twin you an' your cash,
>   But scant this day.
>
> Here cantin varlets, thrawn an' cross,
>   Wi' ballad singers skirl:
> There blackguard boys at pitch-an-toss,
>   Gar baw-bees crimbly birl;
> There's ginge bread wives and tinkler jades,
>   In garbs o' monie a texture,
> With folk o' a' kinds, callins, trades,
>   Mak' up the motley mixture
>   That's here this day!

From 'The Summer Fair' in *New poems* (Belfast, 1799).

However, Belfast was rapidly becoming the chief centre of commerce for the neighbourhood. During the eighteenth century the roads were developed. Carts not only carried produce from the fields, but, increasingly, flax and linen. Linen was produced in cottages and farms all over the countryside and valuable bleach greens were established in the Carnmoney neighbourhood. At Whitehouse the first cotton mill was established by Nicholas Grimshaw in the 1770s. There were calico printers in Ballyhenry and Mallusk, spinning mills at Mossley, Whitehouse, and Whiteabbey. Cotton launched these mills but it was linen which allowed their tremendous expansion in the nineteenth century. David Biggar, a relative of the McKinneys, organised the Mossley mills.

As regards education, it is interesting to note that when the call was made to the Rev. John Thomson in 1730 to become Presbyterian minister of Carnmoney, not one out of 155 names was signed with a mark but in 1767 when the call was made to his nephew, also the Rev. John Thomson, eight out of the thirty-seven were signed by a mark and not their own signatures. Perhaps earlier signatories were first generation Scots who had benefited from a good education system in Scotland, while poor facilities in Ireland caused illiteracy among their children. In the middle of the century there was a school run by the rector at Carnmoney and possibly

Crambo Cave, the home of Samuel Thomson, April 1902 (W.McK.). Thomson had lived in the front section of the house, which also contained the schoolroom where he taught and two labourers' dwellings.

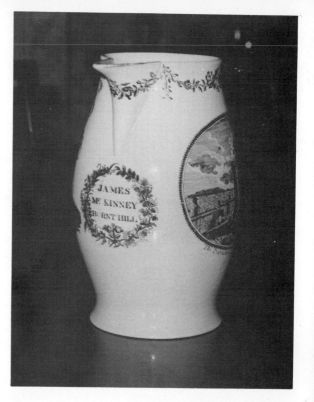

James McKinney's jug celebrating
the Fall of the Bastille (H.C.).

the Presbyterians also had a school. But education does seem to have declined. (William McKinney believed that the Rev. John Thomson had actually deliberately discouraged the establishment of new schools in the late eighteenth century, out of fears that the buildings would be used as meeting-places for secret societies.) Educational facilities did begin to improve in the nineteenth century, although it should be noted that while 232 boys attended Carnmoney parish school in 1821, only 24 of their sisters accompanied them.

See Clarke, *op. cit.*, p.207.

According to the 1766 census figures there were 450 Protestants and 6 Catholics in Carnmoney parish, which made it one of the most Protestant areas in the country. Most of these were Presbyterian. The Presbyterian session meetings continued to regulate the religious and moral code of their members. Although its parishoners were a minority in Carnmoney, the Church of Ireland was the established church and the parish vestry played an important role in various public matters, such as road repairs, care of orphans and schooling. The McKinneys and their relations, in spite of being Presbyterian, served on the vestry. The rector was also entitled to tithes, a source of considerable annoyance to those who did not belong to the Church of Ireland.

During the last decades of this century important political developments occurred which affected the McKinneys. The spirit of political and social reform which arose from the American and French revolutions created a strong radicalism in the north of Ireland. A jug at Sentry Hill, bearing the legend *James McKinney, the Burnt Hill*, and commemorating the Fall of the Bastille, is evidence of the feeling which such events created. People in Carnmoney were actively involved in the reform movement of the 1780s and 1790s. William McKinney later noted down how both of his grandfathers became involved in the United Irish Society which, in face of stern action by the government and a refusal to grant reforms, turned into a secret revolutionary movement.

> The name of my mother's father was Hugh Giffen amd my father's John McKinney. They both joined the United Irishmen who at first only united to insist on reforms being made in the existing government, without any intention of fighting. After William Orr and other innocent men were executed preparations for fighting were commenced.

Hugh Giffen had no part in the rebellion of 1798. From evidence of several persons, McKinney discovered that his other grandfather played a brief but significant role.

> He kept a good horse and was fond of riding and racing . . . An old man named James Bell who lived beside the Roughfort told me that he saw my grandfather galloping past his house three times on the day of the Battle of Antrim and the last time that he saw him he was riding bareheaded. My father told me about his father riding to Antrim to warn the people about the soldiers being on their way marching from Belfast and on the way back he met the soldiers at Templepatrick. He then dismounted, climbed over the wall into Lord Templeton's demesne and came home on foot. The horse was so tired that the soldiers, after taking him a little way allowed him to go free again and he was brought home by somebody.

William McKinney believed his grandfather was the emissary alluded to in McSkimin's history of the rebellion, who carried the order to rise to the United Irishmen at Roughfort and later warned them of the approach of the military. John McKinney survived the rising without any harm but Samuel George, the brother of his future wife, was killed at the Battle of Antrim. Another relative, a second cousin, Samuel Neilson, was a leader of the United Irishmen. Rev. William Steele Dickson, also a prominent member of the society, was born and brought up in Ballycraigy, only a few yards from Sentry Hill.

Interesting information about the well-being of this farming community in the early nineteenth century can be gleaned from the collection of wills at Sentry Hill, mainly acquired because various members of the family acted as executors. For example, in a will dated 1815, John McWhinney of Ballyduff, Carnmoney, bequeathed to his son the house and lands he held under Dr Haliday, together with all his stock. His wife was instructed to live with the son, although if she married again, she was to get £20 and 'the bed she lies upon', and was to leave the farm. If the son died, the farm was to be passed on to the eldest surviving sister. McWhinney left £10 to each daughter, to be paid on her twenty-first birthday, or when she married. One daughter was also to receive a silver watch. He wanted his sister to reside with the family, although if she liked she could live 'in the carr house'. She was to be given £4. 11s. per year, four boxes of turf, two boxes of sods and four quarts of flax seeds, sown, every year. No turf or wood

In the Name of God Amen

I James Murphy of Ballyveasy parish of Carnmoney and County of Antrim Householder being weak of body But of A Sound and perfect Memory praise be to Almighty God for all his Mercies, Do Make and ordain My Last Will and Testament in manner and form as following

Imprimis I leave and bequath my loving wife Mary Murphy my Dwelling house and Garden with every Article of Furniture Cow and Clock with every property Whatever that I may Die possessed of for her use and Benefit During her Natural life or Chaste Widowhood and in Case of her Marriage or at her Decease I Bequath the Room on the South end of the House and the third of the Garden to Elisabeth Agnes and Maria and in Case the Cannot Agree I Alow the Said Room and that part of the Garden Alloted to them to be equaly divided Betwixt them I Bequath the Kitchen to my son James with the one third of the Garden, I Bequath to My Son Samuel the Room on the North end with the one third of the Garden, I Bequath to my Son John £3 pounds or, 16 feet in the Clear on the Ground in front of the house free for ever
if any of My Children should be Dissatisfied with this My Will and put the rest to any trouble the shall forfit their Claim by So Doing
I alow no part of My property to be Sold out of family to any stranger whatever but if any one or more wishes to Dispose of their part it Must be to either A Brother or Sister

I nominate and Appoint Thomas Ferguson of Ballycraigy parish of Carnmoney and Robert Kennedy of Ballyveasy and parish of Carnmoney My Carefull Executors to see My Corpse Decently interd in Mallusk Buring Ground and to See this My Last Will and Testament into effect and force Given under My hand and Seal this 10th of Feburary 1834 and thirty four

was to be cut, except for family use.

Other wills are similar. Normally the farm is left to a son, although it might be divided between several sons. The wife is looked after but the will usually takes a strong line on her possible remarriage. The main item of furniture mentioned is the bed; others include clothes presses, clocks and silver spoons. Often children were left particular rooms in the house, a move obviously intended to ensure that they were not put out by whoever inherited the home.

Occasionally conditions of future behaviour were stipulated. In 1825, after leaving his farm to his son, Henry, Robert Morrow of Ballyvesey bequeathed to his wife and daughter 'the three fields which lie on the north end of my farm together with the kitchen and lower room of my dwelling house and the barn and cow house and half of the garden'. They were to be allowed to go through his son's land 'for the purpose of getting water and of drawing their cattle to and from the watering place'. Morrow also specified:

In case my son Henry should marry Elizabeth Walker, who lately lived servant with me I do hereby order and allow that he shall hereafter enjoy no part of my land or houses but that the same shall revert to my wife and daughter.

Another will worth quoting is that of Dr Alexander Haliday, one of the principal middlemen in the area. After mentioning the larger interests which he bequeathes to his wife, he leaves her '£100 by way of atonement for the many unmerciful scolds I have thrown her way at the whist table', and a further £100 in acknowledgement of her goodness in

> devoting an hour or two every evening, which she could have so much better employed, to amuse me with a game of picket when we happened to be alone, after my delayed eyesight could no longer enable me to write or read much by candlelight.
> ... I leave my copy of Voltaire's works to my amiable and excellent sister-in-law, Miss Dalmonia Edmunstone, as a testimony of my warm esteem, and as she has taste and feeling to relish the beauties of that uncommon genius, so she has too sound a judgement to be perverted by his errors.

Quoted in George Benn's *History of Belfast* (Belfast, 1877), pp.521–2.

Before turning to look at events at Sentry Hill after the marriage of Thomas George and Isabella McKinney in 1831 it will be valuable to look at the Ordnance Survey Memoir which was written for the Carnmoney parish in the late 1830s. This was part of a proposed grand survey of Ireland which was never completed, and the very detailed account of Carnmoney has never been printed before. It provides an excellent view of the community around Sentry Hill in this early period, and is worth quoting at some length.

Housing in the area was described as follows:

> The cottages of the farmers seldom exceed one storey in height. Some of those of more recent erection are two storeys high and are slated but the majority of the farm houses or cottages are roofed with thatch. They are in general low and rather small and there is a want of compactness and comfort in their external appearance. They are however dry, substantial and warm being well built of stone and lime and roughcast. They usually consist of 3 and sometimes of 4 apartments which with the better description of farmers are neatly and sometimes handsomely furnished, and display in their parlour and in one or two bedrooms, considerable knowledge of and attention to taste and comfort but in general their interior arrangement is in perfect keeping with the character and habits of their owners, evincing little regard for taste, almost as little for neatness, but possessing a certain degree of comfort and substance . . .

The writer also commented on the farm outhouses:

> In the construction of their offices and in their arrangement there is a want of regularity. They generally are attached to and form a continuation of the dwelling house. Along their front a narrow and ill-paved causeway extends and beyond it are usually receptacles for the manure from the stable and cow house. Attached to each house is a small and badly enclosed garden in which some early potatoes, cabbages, leeks and onions are raised. The consumption of vegetables is however but trifling and there is very little taste for gardening or planting, a few old ash trees growing about each house constituting its only shelter. There is altogether a want of economy in everything connected with their domestic matters whether as regards the construction of their dwelling or the management of their affairs.

Homes of the labourers and cottiers were also built of stone and lime and were well thatched and warm.

FARMERS' Association.

WE the undersigned Farmers, residing in the Parish of CARNMONEY, HIGH-TOWN, and MALLUSK, being determined as far as in our power, to bring to condign punishment, all Persons who may be guilty of committing any depredation on the property of any of us; do for that purpose form ourselves into an ASSOCIA-TION for Seven Years from this date.

AND in order to give effect to this our determination, we have entered into a Subscription in order to raise a Fund for vigorously prosecuting all Thieves, Robbers, and Receivers of Stolen Goods—And we will put into the Hands of Mr. JAMES M'MILLEN, our Treasurer, a certain proportion of our Subscriptions, for the purpose of liberally rewarding any information that may lead to the discovery and conviction of any Person or Persons who may commit any depredation on the Property of any of us; and for the discovery and conviction of any Receiver of Goods stolen from us—and also for defraying the expences of prosecutions—We will also thankfully receive and liberally reward, such private information, as may lead to the discovery and conviction of any such Thief, Robber, or Receiver of Stolen Goods. The magnitude of the Reward to be proportioned to the importance of the information, and names kept secret if desired.

AND we do now appoint JAMES M'MILLEN, ANDREW SMYTH, JOHN THO-BURN, JOSEPH M'GAW, JAMES HILL, HUGH GIFFEN, SAMUEL FARQUHAR, SAMUEL FULTON, NATHANIEL BOYD, GEORGE WHITE, jun. and WILLIAM BIGGAR, a Committee, to carry our intentions into execution—To any of whom informations may be given, and who will authorise our Treasurer to reward such information.

AND we do further pledge ourselves to each other, that we will individually, in our respective neighbourhoods, use every exertion to prevent any suspicious looking persons from lurking about, without giving a satisfactory account of themselves; and that we will be prepared, as far as possible for repelling any attack that may be made on any of our Houses or Property by Night; and that we will compel every person we may find about our Houses at an unseasonable hour, to account satisfactorily for his or her being there.

Dated 1st May, 1812.

N. B. The Subscribers Names may be seen in the hands of Mr. ANDREW SMYTH, Secretary to the Association.

A. MACKAY, PRINTER, BELFAST.

Announcement of the inauguration of a local farmers' association, 1812, similar to many others established at this time to deal with crime. Eventually a national police force was formed to cope with these problems.

They are in general rather small, the majority of them consisting of but one apartment which is partially divided by a low sod wall reaching about half-way across the cottage. They are pretty well lit by two or sometimes three lead windows. They are generally smoky, the smoke not unfrequently in consequence of the bad construction of their chimneys, making its exit by the door. Their floors are earthen and very frequently damp.

In some cases these labourers lived in the cottages of their employers but in other cases they paid rent for the cottage and a garden and worked for various farmers or in places such as the limeworks. By this period there was little cottage industry.

Regarding the state of agriculture in the parish and the industry of the people, the writer of the Memoir was not complimentary, stating that as the farmers had a good trade in selling buttermilk and butter to Belfast they paid little attention to cultivating or improving their land. After delivering their goods to the town in the morning they spent the rest of the day 'in a half active state loitering about the doors or looking after the cattle'. Only where landlords had put up the rents was there a determined effort to improve the farm. 'In their circumstances they were pretty comfortable but at the time there are not in the parish half a dozen farmers who could command £50 of ready money.'

He went on to make some interesting comments about their ways. 'In their habits and character the people, that is the natives of the parish, are essentially Scottish . . . They are blunt, honest and respectable class, very independent in their notions, particularly on the subject of religion and practical in their engagements.' Their accents he described as strong and broad; 'their idioms and names are strictly Scottish'. They did not 'interfere in party politics'. He also made the remark that:

> There is scarcely a tradition in the parish. This is not much to be wondered when it is remembered that but two centuries have elapsed since their ancestors first settled in the country. But it is rather surprising that scarce a farmer can tell how even his father or grandfather came into possession of the farm on which he dwells.

Morals were on a par with those of neighbouring parishes: 'they are rather fond of whiskey drinking' – indeed there were eighteen spirit shops in the parish, outside the towns, the Memoir records. For neighbouring Donegore it had been observed that:

> To a casual observer their morality and apparently strict observance of the Sabbath would appear striking. They are regular in their attendance at their meeting houses, where in summer they hear two services, with an "intermission" of about half-an-hour between them. But this half-hour, as well as another or two after service, are by the majority spent in the alehouse, an establishment almost invariably to be found in the immediate vicinity of the northern places of worship. With this exception the Sabbath is most properly observed.

In the case of Carnmoney however the Memoir noted:

> there is another species of immorality to which from habit they are quite reconciled and which among themselves, does not bear the same character or appellation as is most commonly applied to it. It is by no means an unusual circumstance that intercourse should have taken place between two parties previous to their being united by the bond of matrimony. In this custom, strange as it may appear, there is an ulterior motive on the part of both. On the woman's that she may compel her father to avoid exposure to make such a settlement on her as will ensure her marriage and on the man's who frequently for sometime refuses to consent, that he may obtain from her father a larger dowry. It is alleged that this is the common motive which in most cases of the kind influences both the parties nor is such an affair by any means held as disreputable.

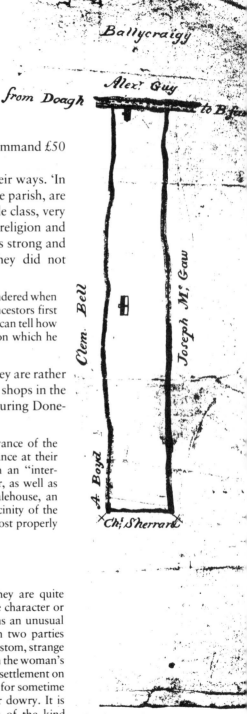

This drawing from a lease kept at Sentry Hill shows John Moreland's farm in Ballyvesey at the time of this report.

The writer of the Memoir also drew attention to their 'remarkably superstitious' nature: 'In no part of Ireland does a more implicit belief exist in witchcraft, sorcery or the black art as also in fairies, brownies and enchantments.' He recorded the instance of a case in 1807 in the area when an attempt by a 'well known sorceress' to cure a sick cow led to the accidental death of three persons. He noted also that there were still twenty-three 'gentle bushes' (fairy thorn trees) in the parishes: 'These as well as the old rafts [raths] are held in great reverence and their demolition or mutilation is considered as sacrilegious.'

A useful account is given of the dietary habits of the population:

Potatoes constitute the great basis of food for all classes. The farmers live frugally and roughly. The animal food which they almost daily consume being chiefly confined to salt pork or bacon, beef being, except by a few rarely used. During summer when potatoes are old and scarce meal made into stirabout and into cakes, is in common use. Salt herrings, broth made of vegetables with a little meat boiled in it, milk and eggs, constitute the food of the farmers. Tea is in more general use among them than formerly as is also baker's bread, the facilities for procuring both being now much greater.

Among the cottagers including the agricultural labourers and those employed at the manufactories, potatoes are the great article of consumption. The agricultural labourers generally grow a sufficient quantity to supply their family upon ground which is given to them gratis for the purpose and upon which they spread their manure.

The kitchen at Sentry Hill, 1980 (D.D.). Some nineteenth-century horn spoons and butter pats can be seen on the table.

21

Dress is also described:

The costume of all classes on Sundays and on public occasions is not merely neat and respectable but is of an excellent description well finished and selected and disposed with no little share of taste. This is particularly the case with the females of the better class whose appearances on these occasions is exceedingly interesting. To observe them when going to or returning from their places of worship would impress an idea of wealth and affluence that does not exist but still there is nothing gaudy or paltry in their attire. During the week the costume of all classes is plain and homely; that of the men and of the females of the lower class is almost slovenly. The children of the cottagers are in a state of partial nudity and are also filthy and untidy but still there is more attention to cleanliness in the persons of the men and women than their appearance would indicate.

Their amusements were given as dancing, quilting and attending singing schools: 'card playing and cock fighting . . . have been almost entirely given up'. The Memoir for the neighbouring parish of Templepatrick had noted that in manners the people were 'uncivil and uncouth. They rarely say "Sir" to or salute their superiors, no matter how dependent on them.' For Carnmoney, however, it was stated that they were more courteous than formerly: 'They are now civil and obliging and are humane and charitable.' The people were described as shrewd: only a few subscribed to newspapers and the 'general taste for knowledge is confined'.

Finally we can observe the writer's comments about the looks of the people:

In stature the men generally exceed the middle size and are pretty well made. They are sinewy and hardy and are capable of under-going much fatigue.

The women are not generally good looking. Their complexion as also their hair is dark, their eyes are either greyish or brown. Their expression of countenance is ruddy and healthy but by no means feminine. They are rather tall but their figures are by no means graceful or light.

For the writer's sake it was just as well perhaps that his observations were not published at the time!

Some caution should be exercised in using the report – enquiries were conducted over a fairly short time and so were not as thorough as might be desirable. For example, we learn from William McKinney's researches that most of the farming families of Scots descent came from Scotland *after* the revolution of 1688–90 and were not descended from the seventeenth-century settlers mentioned above. The report is nonetheless an invaluable survey of the rural society into which William McKinney was born and which was to change radically during his lifetime.

2
Houses and Hobbies

O aughteen hunder and thretty ane,
An hour or twa, an' then thou'rt gane,
To rest for aye, thy weary wings
Among the wreck o' by gane things
And in Oblivion's gulf sae deep
Wi' a thy great forbears to sleep

Samuel Walker, 'Address to the expiring year',
composed and written on the evening of 31 December 1831.

The passing of the year 1831 saw Thomas George and Isabella McKinney master and mistress of Sentry Hill. From a drawing on the 1826 lease for the property we know that their first home was a two-storeyed thatched cottage. It was in this house that William Fee McKinney, the first of their ten children, was born on 21 October 1832. Work began on another house on 23 June 1835, and two months later it was slated, but it was not until 1 December 1836 that they moved into their new dwelling. A photograph of 1870 shows this house as a solid Georgian farmhouse with a fanlight over the front door and glazing bars on the windows.

Information about the house and family in these early days comes mainly from an account book for 1831 and a wages ledger for 1835. The first of these gives an unexpected insight into Thomas McKinney's activities and interests. It lists purchases that one might expect from a farmer – a scythe, a spade, lime, bran, flaxseed, and whiting (for whitewashing) – and a wide range of goods for the house, such as earthen dishes, soap, groceries, saltpetre (for gunpowder), sugar, pepper, herrings, candles, spoons, a bedstead, and cloth for trousers and sheets. Wages are given to labourers on the farm and money is paid out for temporary assistance on jobs such as ditching, stone breaking, potato gathering and corn weeding, as well as kettle mending and clock cleaning.

Sometimes, however, the accounts give interesting hints of his habits. A number of entries for whiskey indicate that he was not averse to a drop of the 'fiery fluid'. He pays to go to dances, to fairs and subscribes to a book club. Clearly he is not one of those whom the Ordnance Survey Memoir described as having a confined taste for knowledge: he buys a book of poetry by Thomas Beggs, an almanac, newspapers, a *Confession of Faith* and makes a quarterly subscription to *The Belfast Magazine*. He is obviously concerned about his appearance, purchasing a waistcoat, pearl buttons, a hat and 'cloth for a coat and trimmings'. We can note the various dues of the day which he regularly pays – turn-pike charges for the use of the main roads, county cess (the contemporary equivalent of today's rates), tithes, church stipend dues, rent, and very substantial interest to Samuel Biggar and Hugh Giffen (probably for the money he raised to purchase his lease).

Drawing of the Sentry Hill farmhouse from a map attached to the 1826 lease.

The account book also reveals the improvements which he introduces to Sentry Hill. The 1500 thorn quicks bought on 15 January 1831 were used to hedge the new ditches he was having made in the fields. In 1831 he buys various trees for Sentry Hill – large quantities of Scotch firs, ash, Lebanon cedar, sycamore, poplar, and beech trees. Many of these can still be seen in the grounds today. Apple trees were also bought to start an orchard. A purchase of flower pots suggests he had more of a liking for flowers than others in the neighbourhood. Through the accounts we also learn where the money for these goods and developments is coming from. Buttermilk, butter, and potatoes are the products which he sells regularly, but cash comes in as well from the sale of flax, eggs, and turf; occasionally a young cow is sold. Rents from labourers for cottages on his land supplement his earnings.

The wages ledger for 1835 contains clues about the people working around Sentry Hill. There is information about the wages of each individual (usually paid after a six-month period of service), with a list of deductions for which money has been specially given out during this time. In the case of Moses Toland, for example, his wages from 12 May to 12 November 1835 were £4.4s.0d, but money was deducted during these months for potatoes, coal, the mending of shoes, and tobacco; the largest

Front view of Sentry Hill, taken in June 1870, by a professional photographer called Hale from Belfast. He came out to Ballyvesey to photograph the McKinneys and their neighbours. When the firm went bankrupt the following year, William purchased a number of his negatives of the area.

Rear of house, 1870 (H.).

sum subtracted was 12 shillings to 'Margaret'. From this evidence it is likely that he lived nearby with his wife Margaret, perhaps in a McKinney cottage. William Sheals, who was paid a mere £1.10s.0d for six months, was probably only a boy servant who lived at the farm – one deduction is 3s.0d. for his mother. It seems clear in the case of Agnes Purvis that she lived on the farm, as there are no deductions for food or rent, and that she was a full-time able-bodied servant or labourer since she is paid £3.0s.0d. It appears also from the list of purchases that she was young and cut a pretty figure!

Agnes Purvis – wages from the 12th May 1835 to 12th November 1835 – £3.0.0.

		£	s.	d.
May 21st	Cloth for Ribband [ribbon]		2	3½
	Silk handkerchief		2	3
	Bonnet Cleaning		1	0
	Worsted and knitting		0	10
	Combs and singing [singeing]		0	6
Oct 1st	Petticoat 3s.4d, bedgown 2s.4d		5	8
26th	In Belfast		4	0
Nov 1st	For a Chest		10	0
		1	6	6½

28th	Handkerchief		0	6
	Calico		2	3
	Worsted and knitting			2½
		Paid	£1 10	0

The family archives give few personal details about Isabella McKinney. What ideas she brought to the building of the new house or its decoration we do not know. One effect she did have, however, was to widen the circle of friends and relations involved with Sentry Hill. Unlike her husband, who had no brothers or sisters and few relations, Isabella had numerous relatives in the neighbourhood. Her mother came from the prolific Biggar family, whose members included J.G. Biggar, the home rule MP, and F.J. Biggar, the antiquarian. Isabella had several brothers and sisters. One brother, William, married a Jane Fee. When he died he left his nephew, William McKinney, a clock belonging to the Fee family, and a small glass with 'William Fee' engraved on it. The clock and glass are still at Sentry Hill. William Giffin had a deep interest in family histories so perhaps this is where William McKinney acquired his concern for the subject.

A Love Letter.

Dear Sarah Jane, you've often said
That, whun a went tae see Belfast
A ocht tae get my picter taen,
So, dear, a've got it tuk at last.

The card it's on is terble nice,
Altho' my face is rether plain ;
A niver wud a got it din,
But jist to please my Sarah Jane.

The man a seen was very kin',
He made me kame an' brush my hair ;
Then tuk me to a darlin' room,
An' set me in a cushined cher.

The wa's wur a wi' picters hung—
A niver seen as nice a place—
And luking glesses here an' there,
A spose tae let me see my face.

He then brocht oot a nice wee box—
My ! thon maun be a cliver man—
Sez he : " Sit studdy, if ye pleese,
An' luk as pleesint as ye can."

A thocht o' *you*--that made me lauch :
The man stud waitin' for a minit,
An' when he cuvered up the box,
He said he had my picter in it.

He sent it till me thro' the post,
Young Jemmy Saunners brocht the letter ;
A hope ye'll be as pleesed as me,
Acause nae picter cud be better.

Noo ye maun get yer likeness taen,
Be shair an' no mistak the hoose
A'll gie ye the address at fut,
Because nae ither's ony use.

ADDRESS :

WILLIAM ABERNETHY,

PHOTOGRAPHER,

29 High Street (opposite Bridge Street),

Belfast.

TO THE WORKHOUSE MASTER—BELFAST UNION.

ADMIT

Name, Surname, and Age of Applicant, his wife, and children under 15, dependent on them.	Andrew Kerr aged 83 years
If Adult—Single, Married, Widower, &c. If Child—Orphan, Deserted, or Bastard.	Widower
When last in Workhouse, and when did leave same.	about six weeks ago
Employment or Calling.	Labourer
If Disabled, description of Disability.	Old age
Whether urgent cases, Observations.	no place of residence
Names and Callings of Relations liable and able to assist Applicant, if any.	None
Where last Resident, and how long?	In Workhouse mostly since February 185
Electoral Division of	Carnmoney Townland of Ballyvesey

NOTE.—The Wardens are particularly requested not to grant an Order for Admission into the Workhouse for any Able-bodied Applicants, for any Women deserted by their Husbands, nor for Children deserted by their Parents, but to send all such Applicants to the Relieving Officer of the District.

Dated this 11th day of February 1856   Signed, Thomas G. McKinney Warden.

Thomas McKinney was appointed in 1841 as one of the wardens of the poor for the Carnmoney division of the Belfast Poor Law Union. This meant he could put forward applications for entry to the workhouse.

Other Giffin relatives kept close contact with Isabella and her new family. Her brother Samuel was a surveyor and contractor who had been responsible for constructing the famous Antrim coast road. In the mid 1830s, perhaps to help the young couple, he took on his brother-in-law as a partner in some road works around Carnmoney. Again in the late 1840s he engaged McKinney and the young William, then aged sixteen, to assist in building a new road from Ballymena to Portglenone – their job was mainly to deal with the accounts and check the men's time. In a diary entry for 30 June 1848, William notes that he and his father walked that day from Ahoghill, where they had lodgings, to Sentry Hill – a distance of over twenty miles.

Two years after the birth of William, a daughter, Jane, was born. Eight more children followed, although the last of these, Eleanor, died shortly after her birth in 1851. They all went to local schools for their early education and then to various educational establishments in Belfast. Because Sentry Hill was a fair distance from Belfast for a child to travel every day, the normal practice was for them to stay in lodgings in the town. An exception to this was William, who was sent only to local schools, perhaps because in his childhood the family was not yet prosperous enough to send him to Belfast; perhaps also it was felt that as the eldest son his future lay at home on the farm and so there was no point in further education in the town.

For the others it was different. John, the second son, attended Belfast Academy and then at the age of sixteen was apprenticed to the provisions'

Far left: Studio portrait of Thomas George and Isabella McKinney, by J. Mack of Belfast, *c.*1880.
Left: Advertisement for the photographic studios of William Abernethy.

Sampler by Margaret McKinney at Sentry Hill, 1980 (D.D.).

business of Edward Coey in Belfast. A fee of £50 was paid by his parents before he started there and they also undertook to pay a further £100 at the end of his five-year apprenticeship. After a time he returned to Sentry Hill, married a neighbour's daughter, Isabella Burney, and set up home on another farm in the vicinity at Sandy Knowes, before leaving with his family for New Zealand in 1877.

The two youngest sons were sent to the Royal Belfast Academical Institution. Hugh eventually studied engineering at the Queen's Colleges in Belfast and Galway; he later went to India and to Australia where he specialised in canal and irrigation engineering. Samuel qualified as a doctor and after some time abroad set up medical practice in London.

The girls likewise were educated at local schools and then in Belfast. On 1 August 1855 William writes in his diary, 'Eliza came home with me from town; she has been six months at Mrs Darley's school in Rosemary Street and has received prizes for grammar and astronomy. She is now going to learn housekeeping.' However, Elizabeth died when she was only eighteen and Margaret, who contracted TB, lived only seventeen years. Isabella married Thomas Archbold of the Bog House, Ballywonard, and they lived on at this address with their family. Sarah's husband, W. J. McGaw, came from Sunnyside farm, only a few fields away from Sentry Hill, and in 1870 they went to Australia where they acquired great wealth and lands.

Jane, the second eldest child, first went to Miss Henderson's day school in Belfast and then qualified as a teacher. For Jane, however, the future did not lie in distant lands. She gained a teaching position in the local school at Carnmoney and fell in love with and married the principal, John Gibson, from Glenavy in Co. Antrim. They were married on 12 November 1855, in the Presbyterian church at Carnmoney. The event was afterwards described by Mary McGaw, one of the bridesmaids, in a letter to a friend, Annie Magill.

There were sixteen present at the ceremony which took place at 12 o'clock. They had four outside cars as Mrs McKinney would not allow them to hire any, and outsiders were the only kind they could borrow. We were only about an hour away; I think they would have taken a ride, but there was some rain while we were out, which prevented that.

After the wedding all returned to Sentry Hill for celebrations. After dinner we went up to the hill and amused ourselves with William's spyglass till we got cold enough. After tea William recited and I sang and we had games and ate apples and other fruit. Bella and Sarah sang too, and so we got on until midnight when we separated, quite tired laughing.

. . . Jane looked remarkably well: she wore a dark silk dress with white ribbon bracelets and belt, ribbon and bow, a little opera cloth of a beautiful shade between lavender and drab, with white lining and ribbon on the hood, and a splendid white bonnet and veil. Eliza and I got striped dresses of silk and wool which we wore with our little drab capes and white bonnets.

Jane and John Gibson set up home in a rented house near the school. In September their first child was born but lived for only four months. Not long afterwards John was taken ill and died on 27 July 1857. Jane then returned to Sentry Hill. The following year, however, she went to a training college in Dublin to obtain further teaching qualifications. Some of her letters from Dublin have survived. One letter, which is undated except for the day, shows well her religious background.

Dublin – Sabbath

My dear mother

Perhaps you do not like the date, but I have been very busy today and would like to tell you what I was engaged at. First, then when I awoke this morning, my R.C. dormitory companions were preparing for 7 o'clock mass (three of them were, one was thinking about it). I lifted my Bible and opened it, when one of them said 'Are you at prayers in bed'. I replied by offering to read a story from my book and so pleased were they that not one went out till 8 o'clock, and only two then. The others sat and listened till I was too hoarse to read any more. It would delight you to see the eager earnestness with which they listen, yet not one of them even offers so much as to lay a finger on the book or look into it. I am to read them some more after dinner. Then I was out at the Sabbath school.

The letter also reveals the innate curiosity which she shared with her brother William. On the previous day she had visited the museum and she comments: 'I wish William had been with me to see the minerals and preserved fish; to me the most beautiful objects were two splendid branches of very natural looking flowers composed of shells.'

She did not enjoy her time at the college, finding the food bad and not liking the staff. She looked forward to letters from home. On 25 September 1858, she wrote to her mother, 'I got a letter from home, and one from John giving an account of your harvest home, and informing me that you are all in your usual health'. Complaining that she didn't hear enough from home she urged her mother to persuade her sister Maggie to write: 'tell her to answer my letter, even if she should only say "My dear Jane, you are very annoying to ask me to write" or some such of her common observations, which, by the bye, I hope are getting less pointed.'

She completed her training in Dublin and returned home. She died not long afterwards in November 1861 from TB. A former pupil at her first school, Margaret McComb Scott, wrote a sentimental but touching piece about her short and sad life.

She seemed to pass as quietly away,
As day doth merge on night, or night on day.
At twenty six she died, yet in these years
She had accomplished much, and many tears
Were shed for her, for we knew even then
We never more would see her like again.
And though so many years have passed away
I gather these few leaves and sadly lay
Them now upon her tomb; some one may yet
Bring flowers, sweet flowers fresh and dew wet
And with deft fingers a fair wreath entwine
To lay beside these few green leaves of mine.
But the best, the happiest time was when I with the rest
Would gather round our fair young teacher's chair
For the great mid-day lesson, which with care
We had prepared. She'd listen and explain
What was obscure till all would be quite plain.

The one child of Thomas George and Isabella McKinney whose future has not yet been discussed is, of course, William. He was educated locally at various schools: a later note of his gives a list of eight schools which he attended – this suggests a rather unruly child!

He had disagreements with his father which caused him to leave home a number of times. On 12 September 1851 he notes in his diary that he had

shorn corn in the bogland until dinner time after which my father scolded me for not having shorn enough and took the hook from me and commenced to shear himself. I built turf in the stackyard until 4 o'clock after which I went to Ballynure Road and took the train to Belfast and the steamer, Princess Alice, to Fleetwood.

He went to Morecombe but returned after a month and his father collected him at Belfast. In 1860 he left for Canada but came home fourteen months later. Apart from these brief trips abroad, he lived at Sentry Hill with his parents until his marriage in July 1861.

Some of William's personal account books have survived for this period prior to his marriage and they give a good picture of a carefree bachelor. For example, between August 1854 and August 1855, he pays 6d. to see 'Manders managerie', 1s.6d. for a card to go to a soirée at Lyle Hill, 1s.6d. for tickets for a soirée at Doagh, 30s.0d. for cloth for a beaver coat, 13s.0d. for 'a blue silk blush vest', 4s.6d. for a silk handkerchief and money on

Ambrotype studio portrait of
William McKinney, 1852.

various occasions for bullet moulds and gunpowder. He also purchases a catechism, copies of *The Northern Whig*, the poems of John Ramsay, and 'likenesses' [photographs] of worthies such as the presbyterian cleric and politician, Dr Henry Cooke, as well as relatives. He has his watch cleaned and buys a 'snake in a bottle' for 1s.0d.

In July 1861 he married Eliza McGaw, who lived only a few fields away from Sentry Hill at Sunnyside. William now purchased from her family the Fairymount part of the farm, where they set up home. Over a period of eleven years they had nine children. A letter of Eliza's from Fairymount paints a pleasant picture of their early life together. She describes the children to her friend Annie Magill, but is far from being an uncritical mother:

5th December 1863

My Dear Annie,

How have you been getting along this long time, and how is Miss Magill and your little ones? Many a time I had intended writing you, but there was still something came to prevent me from doing so. I have had a busy time of it nursing since I saw you. We had two children to nurse the most of the summer. The eldest one is getting teeth and has had measles and colds and one thing and another; he has scarcely ever been well for the last three months: he is better now than he has been for a long time. The little one is very fat, people say he is a very big child for his age, but perhaps, they think it pleases me to hear it. His hair is

Mrs Margaret McGaw, mother of
Eliza McKinney, who lived with her
daughter and son-in-law at
Fairymount, 1870 (H.).

very near red. I think it will be brown yet. His face is very pale, mouth very small,
a dimple on his chin and one of his cheeks, high broad forehead and very dark
eyes.

She relates that her mother is living in the house while William that evening
is at a meeting of church stipend collectors: 'The children are sleeping and
all is quietness'.

Eliza then records a piece of scandal about a local girl:

She has taken a fancy for the Rev. Mr Lynd, Whiteabbey. She got a revelation
from heaven that she is to be his wife. She has been annoying him this long time,
but the other day she went to his house and commenced to strip off her clothes
and prepare for the bed, but Mr Lynd was like Joseph, he fled from her, and set
off for the police to take her up. He went rather farther than Joseph did, but she
says she'll be like Paul with perseverance to the end.

Fairymount, *c.*1895 (W.F. McK.). The farm took its name from a nearby mound, popularly believed to have been the residence of a colony of fairies. The bottom rock is shaped like a small chair. The cottage was of the longhouse type and also contained room for the animals.

Only one other piece of writing by her has survived. It is part of a letter begun by William to his brothers at college in Galway in October 1866 which she completed as he was unwell:

Your long and interesting letter arrived here all right. We were very glad to hear of Samuel's good fortune, and hope that you will suceed well at Xmas . . . Our youngsters are all well, Joseph fell into the spout today, he was all wet but his head, which he contrived to keep out of the water. He is nothing the worse. Tell Samuel not to be too severe on the orthography of this epistle as I was in a hurry and I am sure there are mistakes in it not a few. I shall bid you good bye for the present and remain yours affectionately.

E. McKinney

William's account books from the 1870s reflect his new family responsibilities. In 1873, for example, he pays school fees, and 12s.6d. 'to Dr Dundee for attending Eliza'. Other entries include 'shoes for John, 7s.3d.', 'boots for Janet and Margaret, 10s.3d.' and apples, nuts and grapes for Halloween. On 25 July 1873 he notes: 'E [Eliza] and I and the six children in Belfast, seeing Anderson, the Wizard of the North. Tramway drive etc. 6s.0d.'. He pays for a range of household goods and foodstuffs which is undoubtedly wider than his father purchases, forty years earlier – coffee, tins of beef, Australian lamb, cakes and bread. He also purchases postage stamps, a concertina and a looking glass as well as various books and newspapers.

In contrast to his father, William pays no tollgate dues, but he does find himself liable for income tax (and, from the 1870s, for dog tax), as well as the usual county cess, church sustentation and pew-rent money. From the 1830s it was usually the landlords, not their tenants, who paid tithes, but

One of the bills for furniture received by John and Catherine McKinney while setting up their new home at Sunnyside.

because William had a perpetuity lease on Sentry Hill, *he* had to pay the tithes. He also contributes to the foreign missions. In addition to his rent, he also has to meet various interest repayments on loans borrowed to buy Fairymount and to pay for improvements. In 1861 he had received a joint mortgage loan of £600 at 5 per cent interest from his friend Thomas Houston and the company of Joseph Biggar in Belfast; it was not redeemed until 1868. Smaller sums, totalling almost £1000, were borrowed over the period 1861–71 (usually at a lower interest rate) from relatives and from people in the area, such as the McCrums. In the same period he received over £600 from his wife's relatives in Melbourne, partly for the education of the children. He had a bank account in Belfast. Like his father his main source of income was from sales of butter, buttermilk and potatoes, but he also bought shares in various companies, including Arnott's and the Ulster Bank.

Of the nine children born to William and Eliza, one died at birth, but all the others survived – evidence in part of improved medical facilities. A good education was clearly a priority for *all* the children. John went on to the Belfast Royal Academical Institution and then returned to help with the farming. He married Catherine Smith of Mossvale, Hightown, and moved in 1890 to the neighbouring farm of Sunnyside. The other sons were also educated at RBAI but thanks to the expansion of the Belfast tramway system, they were able to travel to school every day. Thomas, Jim, and Joseph emigrated to Australia to join their McGaw uncles. Hugh became a doctor and went to Nigeria. The two daughters, Janet and Meg, went to Miss Robinson's Educational Establishment for Young Ladies on the Antrim Road in Belfast, and then to Queen's College, West Kensington, London, before returning home. Janet married Isaac Dundee, the local doctor in Carnmoney, in 1895. Meg was to live at Sentry Hill for the rest of her life.

Eliza McKinney (1831–1877) and children at Fairymount, 1870 (H.).

Eliza did not live to see her children grow to maturity. Frequently in

Sunnyside, *c.*1892 (W.McK.): Catherine, John McKinney's wife, on the pony and trap, and Miss G. Strahan on the bicycle.

William's diaries there is mention of her being unwell, a fact which was probably related to constant child-bearing. In March 1877 she was taken ill again and died on 3 June. Eliza's death was described by William in an unusually long diary entry:

She was very weak all day and vomited everything that we gave her until two o'clock when John brought home ice from Belfast that Mr McGaw drove in for. We gave her the ice in small lumps which she seemed very fond of. Dr Wilson was here in the morning and evening. Eliza was able to speak little all day, but about half an hour before she died she seemed to revive and her voice became stronger and she began to talk about going to meet her Lord, for she said 'I know that my Redeemer liveth.' The children were in their beds but I awoke them to see her before she departed and she talked to them all. Miss McGaw was the

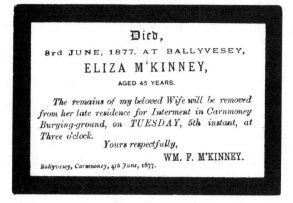

Died,

8rd JUNE, 1877, AT BALLYVESEY,

ELIZA M'KINNEY,

AGED 45 YEARS.

The remains of my beloved Wife will be removed from her late residence for Interment in Carnmoney Burying-ground, on TUESDAY, 5th instant, at Three o'clock.

Yours respectfully,

WM. F. M'KINNEY.

Ballyvesey, Carnmoney, 4th June, 1877.

only person not belonging to the house who was present when she died. She died at twenty minutes past eleven. John drove off with the cart for Jennie Guthrie and Mary Ann who came and dressed her remains.

He then recorded his own sense of personal grief:

... I am now left to wander I know not where. She was my best friend and councillor, my constant attendant, a comforter in every trouble and an adviser whom I could always trust, she was faithful, kind and true.

Family relatives and friends gave valuable assistance to William and his children in the immediate period after Eliza's death. They remained at Fairymount until 1885 when, with his youngest children, he moved back to Sentry Hill which his father had conveyed to him two years earlier for £1500 and where his parents continued to live. In 1884 William conveyed Fairymount to his eldest son John in consideration 'of the natural love and affection' which he bore him. In 1886 T.G. McKinney gave £400 to William as an annuity set against Sentry Hill, from which he received £18 per annum. This no doubt would have satisfied both parties as it gave William the money but allowed his father full security.

The changes which were carried out to the home in 1885–6 were clearly William's work and transformed Sentry Hill from a Georgian farmhouse to a modern Victorian residence. New windows were put in most of the house, with decorative frames around them. A bathroom was added in 1885 as were a kitchen and scullery. An Eagle range was installed in the kitchen to heat water for the bathroom and scullery. The following year a porch was built at the front of the building, with a conservatory above.

In 1886 Isabella McKinney died at the age of eighty and in 1893 Thomas George McKinney passed away in his eighty-sixth year. They left a Sentry Hill and a community which were very different from the home and countryside of their early days. We have few details about their part in all this, as neither kept diaries or records. We do know that he was a ruling elder in his church for forty-five years, and played a prominent part in a local Sabbath school, and as such seems to have been highly regarded. But

The hearth at Fairymount, c.1895 (W.F.McK.). Note the oven on the left and the hot-water boiler on the right.

The morning room at Sentry Hill, 1980 (D.D.). The glazing-bar window with shutters is the only one which survives from the 1835 house. William McKinney often used this small room for writing his historical and geological studies.

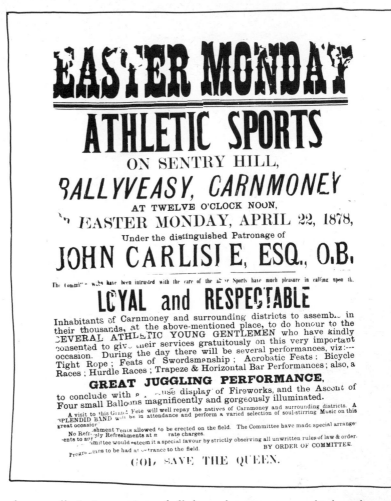

EASTER MONDAY

ATHLETIC SPORTS

ON SENTRY HILL,

BALLYVEASY, CARNMONEY

AT TWELVE O'CLOCK NOON,

ON EASTER MONDAY, APRIL 22, 1878,

Under the distinguished Patronage of

JOHN CARLISLE, ESQ., O.B.

The Committee who have been intrusted with the care of the above Sports have much pleasure in calling upon the

LOYAL and RESPECTABLE

Inhabitants of Carnmoney and surrounding districts to assemble in their thousands, at the above-mentioned place, to do honour to the SEVERAL ATHLETIC YOUNG GENTLEMEN who have kindly consented to give their services gratuitously on this very important occasion. During the day there will be several performances, viz:--- Tight Rope ; Feats of Swordsmanship ; Acrobatic Feats : Bicycle Races ; Hurdle Races ; Trapeze & Horizontal Bar Performances ; also, a

GREAT JUGGLING PERFORMANCE,

to conclude with a grand display of Fireworks, and the Ascent of Four small Balloons magnificently and gorgeously illuminated.

A visit to this Grand Fete will well repay the natives of Carnmoney and surrounding districts. A SPLENDID BAND will be in attendance and perform a varied selection of soul-stirring Music on this great occasion

No Refreshment Tents allowed to be erected on the field. The Committee have made special arrange-ments to supply Refreshments at moderate rate charges.

The Committee would esteem it a special favour by strictly observing all unwritten rules of law & order.

Programmes to be had at entrance to the field. BY ORDER OF COMMITTEE.

GOD SAVE THE QUEEN.

for a really intimate view of all these changes we must look at the papers and diaries which their son William kept. They reflect not just his special character, his activities and interests, but also the changing social, religious, political and cultural ways of the world around Sentry Hill.

Over the years William's activities changed, due to his growing older and to the developments which were taking place in the countryside around him. In the 1850s he and his brothers amused themselves walking, shooting and 'throwing bullets'. In June 1852, for example, he writes that:

Will Carlisle and I went to the turnpike road where a number of men from Hyde Park were throwing bullets. They challenged us to throw with them which we agreed to although neither of us had ever tried it before and we beat their two champions.

After this encouraging start, there were other references to this traditional sport, which involved throwing large metal balls as far up a road as possible. Three years later William noted that on the way out from Belfast, 'there were two men played bullets from the 6th to the 9th milestone at 33 throws for £20 a side. A Paisley weaver beat the Belfast spinning master

John Giffin, William's uncle, 1870 (H.).

(Gibson)'. These matches continued until the 1880s when the police, fearing for the safety of travellers, halted them. John McKinney had his name taken by the police at a bullets competition in 1882.

The diaries also contain references to shooting otters and teal in the neighbourhood, as well as trips to Islandmagee to shoot puffins and other birds. In July 1856 William went with his uncle, John Giffin, his brother John and another friend to the Isle of Muck, off Islandmagee:

> I shot a cormorant. We caught two grey birds lords and a cod fish. The Islandmagee men were catching herrings with geezers. Left Bob Houston's at 11 o'clock; home at half past two.

The next day he skinned and stuffed the cormorant.

Later on shooting competitions were held in local farmers' barns and fields to raise money for various good causes. William's son John fell afoul of the law in the late 1870s, for using his father's gun without a licence. On 21 March 1878 William records:

> Went to Whitehouse Petty Sessions and paid £2.10/- of a fine on account of a popish vagabond of a policeman having seen John with my gun at Mrs McMullan's where he had followed a magpie that he had wounded.

There must still have been some cock-fighting carried on in the area, because in July 1865, William mentioned how some men were tried in the local petty sessions for this offence.

During this time William developed his singing talents. He and his brothers attended singing classes at Monkstown and other places. In 1854 he 'went to O'Hanlon's singing class; the terms are 1s.6d. per quarter'. At this time the organ was not acceptable in most Presbyterian meeting houses, so clearly good singing was important for the services. In some notes on the subject, William explains that for a long time the church music was confined to twelve tunes. When new tunes were introduced around 1814, this innovation caused some members of Carnmoney congregation to leave for other churches: McKinney quotes one such person who later explained to him 'that he would not thole [bear] tae sit an' listen them sing them Lillabullero tunes'. Singing classes were now held in farmers' barns. To help learn the tunes, verses were specially composed for the purpose with the name of the tune generally in the first line. Sometimes people composed their own lines and set them to these tunes:

> When I sat down to take a smoke,
> My pipe was lying empty,
> Thinks I, the man is happy blest
> Who has tobacco plenty.

Although these classes continued throughout the nineteenth century, they became less devoted entirely to sacred music and were seen as means to a social grace and an enjoyable way to pass the time. There were various occasions for singing outside church. For example in 1853, William records attending a party at the McGaws at which there was 'swinging, singing and recitation until near 2 o'clock'. The recitations were varied in their content – William mentions that he recited a few comic pieces at one such gathering. His grandchildren can still recall how he could recite Dickens, Tennyson, Wordsworth, Carleton, and Sir Walter Scott. Robbie Burns was a family favourite.

Dancing was also popular. The Ordnance Survey Memoir of the 1830s had described how

> scarce a month passes without there being a dance in some of the farmers' houses either in this parish or in those immediately adjoining it. Reels, country dances and sometimes quadrills are the usual figures. The violin is the usual instrument but the highland pipes are also sometimes introduced. They dance pretty well and rather lightly. The refreshments consist of punch and biscuits. The dances got up among the factory people are not by any means conducted with the same propriety as those at the farmers' houses.

CONCERT IN CARNMONEY. — A most successful concert has been held in the schoolroom adjacent to the Church at Carnmoney on behalf of the funds of the forthcoming bazaar in May. The chair was occupied by Mr. Andrew Burney, and there was a large and appreciative audience. The programme consisted of pianoforte solos, "Polka de la Reiul," and Fantasia on Avon, Irish Airs, by Miss Jeanie Moore; violin solos, "I Puritani," and Scotch airs, with variations, by Mr. J. C. Manniece. Songs — "The Guadalquiver" and "The Nightingale's Trill," by Miss Wylie; "At Eventide" and "The Little Dutchman," by Miss Meta Jellett; "We met too late" and "Lovett King," by Mr. F. G. Fenton; "The Holy City" and "The Outpost," by Mr. S. W. H. Wylie; "The Shilling" and "Slattery's Mounted Foot," by Mr. Lloyd Campbell; and "Ora Pro Nobis" and "The Heart Bowed Down," by Mr. C. J. Pirrie. Readings— "The Road to Heaven" and "The Signal Box," by Mr. James McCleery. Frequent encores were called for by the audience during the evening, and in most cases responded to. Miss Jeanie Moore and Miss L. Jellett played the accompaniments with much taste. A humorous and original piece in verse, referring chiefly to the bazaar, was read by Mr Thomas Houston, and was very well received. A hearty vote of thanks to the ladies and gentlemen who had contributed to the evening's enjoyment having been proposed in an eloquent speech by Mr. James Speer, seconded by Mr. Thomas A. Archbold, and conveyed by the Chairman, the proceedings were brought to a close by the singing of the National Anthem.

There were dancing classes, though these were not universally welcomed. An entry in McKinney's diary for 1858 refers to a sermon given by the Rev. Joseph Barkley to 'counteract the effect of Mrs Charles's dancing school'.

Quilting parties would also seem to have been a good excuse for having fun, to judge from their frequent occurrence in William's diary. The earlier Ordnance Survey Memoir gives some idea of what might have gone on at these gatherings:

'Quiltings' are also scenes of amusement and mirth. At the house at which the quilt is to be made or sewn, the young women of the neighbourhood assemble to lend their assistance. Invitations are issued to the young men who commence

12. O! Brunswick, but I love thee well, Thy harmony is sweet;

Thou'rt set upon the treble clef In common time complete.

assembling about 12 o'clock. The morning is spent in conversation and the evening in dancing.

Another favourite social gathering was the soirée. These events ranged from small family affairs to large community ones, sometimes to raise money for various causes. Joseph Carson, a weaver poet from Kilpike, in Co. Antrim, described preparations for one such soirée in 1842 in a manuscript poem in William's papers:

T'other night when the sable of nature was spread
And your Poet and spouse had got nestled in bed
With a book in my hand and light at my nose
As my wont is to learn and encourage repose
In sleep the profoundest was closed every eye
And infantile nurture had stilled the last cry
When a voice at my side like the chirp of a cricket
Says Joseph, my dear, did you buy me a ticket?
A ticket, say I, yes, a ticket, says she,
Sure all the men's wives will be at the Soiree.
And tho' I may not be as splendidly dressed,
I can see and drink tea just as well as the rest
All I want to be decent's a single half crown
To buy a respectable cap in the Town
With nine pence or ten pence for ribbon or lace
And I'll pick up my head with the best in the place.
As calm as I could to pursuade her I tried
That the cash for the cap might be better applied.
For instance I told her the money would buy
Some checkers for slips for our own little fry
Or else it would pay as she very well knew
As part of the Bill to the grocer was due.
Well, well, never mind she replied with a frown
But I wish you were always as thrifty in town
The cash would not last very long on your sprees
At 3 pence the pint double X in Magees
At this critical juncture the child gave a squeal

But the very next morning to Arnolds she sped
And yonder's the cap that she bought on her head
But stop, she's not there, like old puss stole away
For she knew very well I had something to say.

Church music tunes, from a
manuscript book at Sentry Hill.

The twelve old tunes. as used until 1835. The names of the tunes are as follows. 1. French. 2. York. 3. London. 4. Elgin. 5. Dublin. 6. Abbey. 7. Newton. 8. Savoy. 9. Martyr's. 10. David's. 11. Mary's. 12. Brunswick. Done out from an old manuscript of 1790. for W. F. McKinney Esq. in 1901. by J. T. McGaw

McKinney records how at one soirée in Carnmoney Meeting House in 1857 there were lectures on Connaught and India; he mentions also that there was bad behaviour at the meeting. The variety of speeches, songs and recitations which went on on such occasions can be seen in this poem copied into one of William's notebooks:

John Kerr (with the fiddle) and family of Ballyvesey, with William John Steel and a Miss McCrum, *c.*1895 (W.McK.).

A Rhyme on our Annual Soirée

Dedicated without permission to the Superintendent and Teachers of King's Moss Sabbath School.

Mr Speer took the chair, with a homely air,
And received a cordial greeting
From scholars and teachers, and amateur preachers
Who had come to swell the meeting.
And he said he was glad that his school never had,
In a better condition been,
Although it was true he had lost a few,
Through wedlock's incessant stream.

44

On our chairman's left hand rose a teetotal man,
Who made a great oration;
He said 'twas quite clear, that whisky and beer,
Were fast destroying the nation;
In his bachelor speech, he tried for to teach
That tea was an excellent drink,
For it made people glad, while whisky made sad,
No matter what tipplers might think.

Sweet Miss Bruce then sang 'bout the bells that rang,
In the glorious Eden above
And her sweet trained voice left no other choice,
But to admire and love.
Then a man of great fame, whose big person and name,
Every schoolboy ought to know,
Said this happy night, to his memory's light,
Brought scenes that had pass'd long ago.

When we got done, with our harmless fun,
Which was both to instruct and amuse,
We then went out, to dander about,
Or take any way we might choose;
Some steered leeward, and some drifted seaward,
On account of ballast being scarce;
But none went home cross, none spoke ill of the moss
So now I shall end my verse

James Wilson
1877

Weddings were also opportunities for meeting 'to make merry', such as the time when William's sister Jane was married and they all returned to Sentry Hill for singing and games. On another occasion, in 1852, he describes 'great rejoicing by members of the bride's unwashed acquaintances. Three loads of whins were burned before the door by way of an illumination'. They were not always without incident. When William Harpur married Jane Moreland in 1872 his mother raised a row in the church, for reasons which remain unexplained.

Many other activities are noted in his diaries – visiting the circus, attending boat and dog races, playing 'literary whist', and writing 'enigmas'. From an early age it is clear that William had a lively, enquiring mind. He later remembered being in Belfast when the first train arrived in 1839. We read of trips to Belfast to see a diarama of a journey around the world, or the launching of an iron ship. On 7 July 1864 he 'went to the Cave Hill and saw Coxwell's balloon rise from the Botanic Gardens [in Belfast] and alight about 6 miles off in Co. Down'. On another occasion he marvels at 'Burney's electric light'. He visits bookshops and builds up his own library. He acquires a stereoscope and invites his friends to see views, local and foreign. There are a couple of references to theatre-going in the early diaries but none in the later ones. As he grew older, religious and moral considerations may have kept him away from what could have been regarded as a rowdy and disreputable pursuit.

He records anything out of the ordinary that occurs in the neighbourhood. In September 1851 he mentions that 'There was a house fell at Ballyclare last night. Seven or eight people were killed and a great number injured; they had assembled to see men mesmerised'.

When the Prince of Wales was married on 10 March 1863 he notes how 'Three tar barrels were burned on my father's hill'. A few years later he went to Derry to see the 12 August celebrations commemorating the closing of the gates by the Apprentice Boys in 1689 against the forces of King James.

In July 1881 it seemed that the free delivery of post to Ballyvesey would end because the volume of mail to and from the area was not high enough. So William set to work: his diary states not only that he 'got letters writen to increase the number', but that on the following day, he 'ordered 1 doz. circulars to be sent from Pat Mullan's to Ballyvesey'. This may have helped, for the delivery of post continued.

There are frequent references to illness in the diaries. Tuberculosis, or consumption, as it was then called, was rampant in the countryside. William's sister Meg lived only seventeen years before she fell victim to what was then a killer disease. In November 1876 William 'went to Thos. Archbold's where Mr Barkley baptized John Archbold's child at the

This rare view of Donegall Place, Belfast, was taken by the Magill Photographic Studio c.1865. Note the buildings at the end of the street: Royal Avenue has not yet been built.

bedside where Lizzie [his wife] is lying in consumption'. Medicine was still in a fairly primitive state of development. Leeches were often used to let blood as this was believed to be beneficial in many illnesses. Even headaches were sometimes treated this way.

Another 'cure', not without its advocates today, was that favoured by Alec. Barkley, one of the farm labourers, who 'drank half a pint of whiskey before he went to bed to cure him of the cold'. According to McKinney, he was still 'unwell' the following morning!

Advances were being made, nonetheless. Vaccination against smallpox was accepted practice for all the McKinney children in the 1860s. Samuel McKinney, William's brother, went to London in the 1870s for an operation at the hands of the famous Lord Lister who was responsible for the development of antiseptics. The development of the dispensary system, which provided medical assistance for those who could not afford to pay private fees, was perhaps the single most important factor in improving the

Carnmoney dispensary, *c.*1900 (W.McK.).

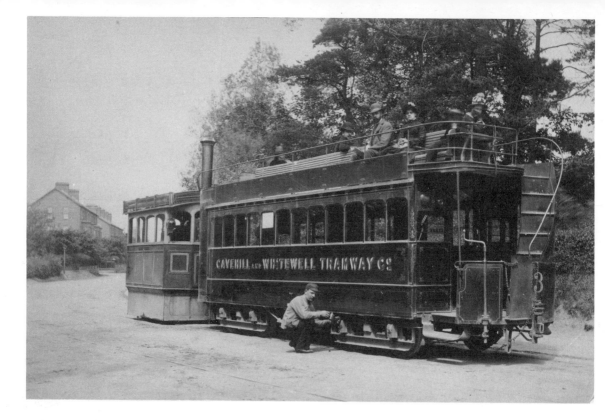

general health of the community. William served for a while on the local dispensary committee, and his papers include canvassing letters from hopeful applicants for the post of dispensary doctor.

The Cavehill and Whitewell Tramway Co. started operations in 1883. The steam-driven tram ran from the centre of Belfast to Glengormley. The service was used frequently by members of the McKinney family. (The photographer is not identified but the photograph was probably taken c.1885.)

3
Faith, Friends and Factions

For William McKinney, religion was the keystone, not only of his beliefs, but also of his activities. Every Sunday he went to church at least once and he taught for a while in the Presbyterian Sabbath school. In 1855, he was elected secretary of the local congregation, a post involving considerable work, which he held for sixty-two years. In this capacity he also acted as secretary to the church committee, which met regularly and was responsible for maintaining the fabric of the church and other congregational buildings. Collecting money was another, very important, function of the committee. Stipend money was raised from each member of the congregation to pay the minister. Pews were rented to families each year, which gave them exclusive rights over them. After 1869 money had also to be gathered for a central sustentation fund. Special funds were collected for the rebuilding of the church in 1856 and the erection of a new lecture hall in 1892. The stables at the meeting house were enlarged to accommodate twenty-six horses and their vehicles under one roof. As secretary William kept the records of how all these funds were collected and these are still to be found in the Sentry Hill collection.

The committee was elected every three years and was always chaired by a layman. Meetings were sometimes controversial, with arguments arising over the allocation of pews or the spending of money. The committee was responsible for the distribution of money to the poor, known as flaxseed money, because at an earlier time flaxseed had in fact been given to those in need. From the early eighteenth century on, the flaxseed contribution had been the main source of charity for the destitute in the area, until 1841, when the workhouse in Belfast offered an alternative but less attractive means of support.

McKinney took a keen interest in all these church activities but the services were the principal interest of his involvement. He kept a notebook with the texts of every sermon he heard during his lifetime. His diaries record visits to other churches to hear different preachers – on one occasion he walked twenty miles to hear Rev. Henry Cooke preach. On 28 December 1856 he writes: 'John Carlisle and I walked to town to hear Mr H[ugh] Hanna. He pointed out some of the leading errors of Romanism and Armenianism.'

His diaries describe the growing religious excitement which later became known as the '59 revival. At first he was sceptical of some of these activities but later he himself had a religious conversion. On 29 June 1859 he attended a service at Ballycraigy meeting house.

NOTICE.

The Collectors will call on the SEAT-HOLDERS during the first week in July for all PEW RENTS due up to that date.

(SIGNED BY ORDER.)

W. F. M'KINNEY,

SECRETARY.

CARNMONEY PRESBYTERIAN CHURCH.

A number of my young friends who seemed unbounded with joy on account of their new born love took me by the hands and asked me if I was happy. I felt most unhappy and told them so. They then told me to pray. I requested a number of them to pray for me which they said that they would do. When I got home to my room at 2 o'clock I knelt down at my bedside and tried to pray to the Lord to have mercy on me but I could not. I then began to shed tears and felt as if my heart was breaking.

Carnmoney Presbyterian church, 1893.

His religious experience continued through the early morning of 30th June.

At half past two o'clock this morning while I was trying to pray I felt as if enveloped in a cloud of horrid darkness and a terrible weight pressed upon my head which made [me] feel as if I was going to be crushed into the earth when suddenly a sound came into my ears and I felt quiet light and happy immediately after the moment that I heard the sound. During the time that I was in the dreadful darkness I cried to the Lord to take me for I felt that I could not go to him myself and that I would be lost if I did not get to him. I said that I was of no use in this world and could do nothing to obtain my own salvation and if he would take me to himself I was willing to go just then. When I heard the sound I thought that the dreadful weight that was trying to crush me into the ground had killed me and I cried to the Lord 'oh take me take me'. After some time I have no idea how long I was aroused by an agreeable tremor in my head and body and felt assured that 'Jesus died for me'.

. . . I went to Mrs McGaw's as soon as I got up; met Eliza and Samuel Easton as I went. They shook hands with me and told me that they knew that I was better and happier. They had been praying for me. Went to Hyde Park with about 100 converts.

The number of seat-holders in Carnmoney Presbyterian church actually declined during the nineteenth century, in spite of a rise in population. This was partly due to the building of new churches in the area and to the amalgamation of farms and subsequent drop in the number of Presbyterian farming families. New labourers moved in to the area to work in the factories but these tended to be Church of Ireland or Catholic.

The religious revival of 1859 was widespread throughout the Ulster countryside but should not be seen in isolation. The minute books of Carnmoney church sessions, the body of elders responsible for the spiritual side of the life of the church, record how by 1859 there had already been a considerable improvement in sabbath attendance, the temperance movement was growing and the practice of 'serving [alcohol]' at funerals had ended.

There were already many sabbath schools in the area, some founded in the early decades of the century: by this time there were seven in the parish and three more in the immediate vicinity. William McKinney had taught in one of these since the early 1850s. But the revival brought an added spiritual dimension to the religious life of the community and these developments carried on at a greater rate than before.

The Presbyterian minister was a regular visitor to Sentry Hill. He is seen here with some of the McKinney family and friends on a visit in 1901. They are (*from left to right*) Meg McKinney, Rev. Hugh Waterworth, Mary Bird, a friend of Meg's, Fergus Wilson (manager of the Blackstaff Mills, Belfast), Tom McKinney, John McKinney (*standing*), Miss Chisolm (of Leigenfield, Mossley), W.H. Boyd (of Carntall) and Elsie McKinney.

William McKinney (*right*) outside Sentry Hill with a neighbour, Charles Scott, who led the singing at Ballycraigy Congregationalist Church for many years, 1910 (W.McK.).

The minutes of the sessions after 1859 show these continuing changes. Strong disapproval is often expressed of drinking alcohol and those known to be given to intemperance are urged by visiting elders to give up their ways. Tracts are spread around the congregation and prayer meetings are encouraged at homes. Great efforts are made to boost church attendance with elders as well as the minister visiting members of the congregation. These changes also seem to have affected sexual morality. By the 1880s very few cases of fornication come before the session. The main task of the session in the last decades of the century is examining young people on the catechism and scriptures, and admitting them to partake in the communion service.

By the time of the revival superstitions were far less widespread than they had been at the time of the Ordnance Survey Memoir in the 1830s, as W. O. McGaw, Eliza's uncle, noted in the 1860s:

> What a great change time has wrought in little more than half a century! The belief in the existence of fairies and witches, brownies and banshees, ghosts, wraiths and hobgoblins, which was at that time almost universal, is now fast dying out – is, indeed, all but extinct.

As regards the substance of William McKinney's beliefs it is clear that he accepted fully the orthodox teaching of his church. The prime importance of the scripture was stressed. The following poem by Thomas Beggs,

Joseph Boyd, local sabbath school teacher, and family, Carnmoney village, March 1901 (W.McK.).

copied by McKinney into a notebook, expresses this high regard for biblical truth:

Acrostic

Written on the fly-leaf of a bible
by Thomas Beggs

Best of treasures, thou art mine
All thy maxims, are divine;
Rich in truth, which maketh wise,
Book of books, "my sacred prize"
All thy words, to me doth prove,
Richest blessings – from above;
Angels, also, prove their love.

Friends of Sinners, is thy name,
Ev'ry page, these truths proclaim;
Robes of glory, all may find,
Gems most pure, to deck the mind;
Unto us, is held to view,
Songs, which sages never knew;
Oh! All mankind, behold; and read;
Now Christ our God, for sinners plead.

How he reacted to Darwin is not obvious. His brother Samuel wrote several books challenging Darwin's theories of creation. His main objection to Darwin was that he failed to allow for the Divine Will and intervention in the creation of man. Samuel was also concerned that Darwin's theories were being used by some to claim superiority of one race over another.

There was great certainty in William McKinney's religious beliefs. He had no doubt that the Presbyterian Church was the true church both in terms of history and in its current practice. Writing on the actions of the seventeenth-century bishop, Jeremy Taylor, who had insisted on the church at Carnmoney being used exclusively for Church of Ireland services, he remarked on 'the nonsensical, unscriptural customs that are still practised in the Epispocopalian church'. He had an even greater dislike for the Catholic Church, which he regarded as wholly unscriptural and dominated by Pope and clergy. Such views were not unique to McKinney. Members of other denominations often adopted similarly exclusive attitudes and during the second half of the nineteenth century all the Irish churches saw the development of a strong, narrow orthodoxy. Religious controversy was also widespread in many parts of Europe at this time but it took on a special significance in Ireland because of the close relationship between religion and politics.

William McKinney took a leading part in the literary and cultural societies of the area, including the Lisnalinchy Debating Society and the Ballycraigy Reading Society. The reading society's books included many on religious subjects, as well as others by Macaulay, Dickens and Burns, and a few on Irish history, such as a life of Henry Grattan.

William's own literary taste was wide. Throughout his life he bought books on a wide variety of topics and at the same time developed certain special interests. He built up a fine collection of the work of the Ulster rural poets of the late eighteenth and early nineteenth centuries. He made the acquaintance of Joseph Semple, who had been a personal friend of many of these poets, and acquired from him a number of their books and letters.

One such poet was Samuel Thompson, a school teacher who lived in a cottage called Crambo Cave (see photograph on p.14) at Lyle Hill, less than a mile from Sentry Hill. He published three collections of verse and prose before his death in 1816. William obtained copies of his books as well as a volume of correspondence (now in the library of Trinity College, Dublin), which reveals Thompson's contact with a wide range of men, including Robbie Burns. He wrote on various subjects such as Roughfort fair, the seasons and different animals.

This extract from a poem about his home suggests that he was genial company but also that he was particular in his choice of friends.

Crambo Cave

Beneath the northern brow of verdant Lyle,
　Where fertile fields with green abundance wave,
Apart from 'dam' rows cities many a mile,
　Appears a rural cot. clep't Crambo Cave

Here Nature simply, in contempt of Art
　A rustic poet to the world gave,
Who, wild as wordlark, plays his tuneful part,
　Beneath the mossy roof of Crambo Cave

Reader, if ever you should pass that way,
　And curiosity sufficient have;
Alert your relish and approve his play
　He'll bid you welcome to his Crambo Cave

But if you know yourself to be an ass,
　A blockhead, thickskulled, narrow, selfish knave,
Quick on your plodding, grappling business pass
　Nor lose one minute in Crambo Cave

But come ye chosen, ye selected *few,*
　Who can be wise and worthy, gay and grave,
The Mutin owner doth soliat you
　To come and see him oft in Crambo Cave.

McKinney was a founder member of the Carnmoney Mutual Improvement Society, formed in 1869. Its objects were 'the promotion of religious, literary and scientific knowledge and co-operation in doing good': political questions could not be introduced at meetings. This society met monthly and papers were read on a variety of subjects. Clearly the tone of these meetings was very different from the type of activities indulged in by earlier reading and debating societies, such as the Four Town Book Club, at whose 'special anniversary' in 1855, he recorded, disparagingly, 'there were no speeches made, but instead there was dining,

drinking, grog and fighting, which is the usual custom when members of the Arian literati are managers'.

Papers read at the Carnmoney Mutual Improvement Society ranged over subjects as diverse as 'The Huguenots', 'Self Improvement', 'Caxton and the Art of Printing', 'Social Reforms' and 'Sir Walter Scott'. McKinney himself spoke on the history of Carnmoney and on the Ulster rural poets. Those papers and notes which survive show a good historical appreciation. He searched out a wide range of material on the history of Carnmoney. His writings were of course coloured by his own opinions, and were in part a response to exclusive claims put forward by Catholic writers. For example, a Father James O'Laverty had written of the lands 'which God intended for the Irish' and which the English and Scots had taken at the end of the sixteenth century in East Antrim. In a lecture to the Society, William McKinney put forward his theory that the Scottish settlers were in fact descendents of former inhabitants of Antrim, the Dalriada Scotti, who had gone to Scotland (and given that country its name), and who had then returned to reclaim their original home. Both arguments had elements of truth and myth.

Apart from the difficulty of proving divine intentions, there was one flaw in O'Laverty's case: the Irish who inhabited this land in the seventeenth century had themselves replaced others. Some of the Scots who came to East Antrim in the 1600s may have been descendents of former Dalriada Scots, but many were not, and certainly the English and Welsh who also arrived could make no such claim; the Dalriada Scots were anyway only one more group which had inhabited the land. Both writers were of course seeking historical justification for their contemporary positions.

In his history of the area, William McKinney made lengthy references, some greatly exaggerated, to the massacre of Protestants in 1641. He dealt very little with the rebellion of 1798, which might seem surprising since his family had fought for the United Irishmen and, indeed, his great-uncle, Samuel George, had been killed at the Battle of Antrim. No doubt there was still something of a folk memory of 1641 but the selection of that event as a significant incident was more influenced by the situation in the 1880s. Because of economic and political developments as well as their feelings about Catholicism, McKinney and his friends would have preferred to remember events that supported their stand for the Union, rather than opposed it.

Temperance was another frequent topic of discussion. It is interesting to note that in the eighteenth and early nineteenth centuries the Presbyterian community did not seem to regard temperance as a special virtue. Thomas Houston, a close friend of William McKinney, read a paper to the Society in the 1880s in which he dwelt at some length on how matters had improved since that time. Amongst accounts of the drinking customs prevalent at births, marriages, christenings, wakes, and especially at ordinations, he gave an account of one ordination dinner in Antrim in

Mrs Houston, wife of Thomas Houston, William McKinney's life-long friend and colleague in the Carnmoney Mutual Improvement Society.

Members of the Houston and McKinney families outside the Houston home at Ashley, Ballyearl, c.1900 (W.McK.).

1820, when twenty-six clergymen and forty-four laymen sat down to a meal at which the costs were as follows:

Dinner for 75 at 4s.6d.	£16.17.6
51 bottles of wine at 6s.6d.	£16.11.6
Whisky punch	£5. 3.4
Waiters &c	£1. 2.9
	£39.15.1

No accounts survive for any ordination dinners at Carnmoney, although Houston did relate the following story of the aftermath of one:

> The schoolmaster, Mr Patterson, and one of the committee, Mr S. Giffen went into the room on the morning after the dinner to arrange the forms for the scholars, when they espied a coat lying on the floor that they supposed at first had been forgotten – imagine their surprise on lifting it when they discovered a young clergyman esconced therein.

By the second half of the nineteenth century, however, the Presbyterian Church and other bodies were actively promoting temperance.

William McKinney would have had ample opportunity to observe the misery caused by excessive drinking. Among his papers are some letters of Thomas Begg, the Mallusk poet. They describe his vain attempts to give up alcohol. In May 1841 he wrote to John Semple.

> My Dear Friend
>
> The storm has blown past for a time and I hope the last time. I am like the dog in hot weather, I must be both muzzled and cloged – perhaps it is best, at least it

John Condy, Carnmoney National School teacher, 1910, pleased with his new bicycle (W.McK.).

must be so taken – I have erred and the penalty has to be paid. I need not say how much I am obligated to you for the deep interest you took on the trying occasion – God forbid that thee or thine may be ever so tried.

The last day of jeopardy in the same way, is come, and past with me, I may well damn the whisky for it has nearly damned me – and yet withal I love it not. I would be glad to know of the little piece that I sent to the News Letter or if you had called on Mr. Sanson, please let me know by the Bearer.

As Colridge says a wiser and a sadder man I have been since I saw you – But the mind will not be for ever depressed and the old even temper will prevail at the last – and now I say farewell, a long farewell to all intemperate habits. I hope to see you soon, and often too – my best wishes to Mrs. Semple and D. Clyde, while I remain in truth and sincerity Dear John, ever yours,

Thomas Beggs

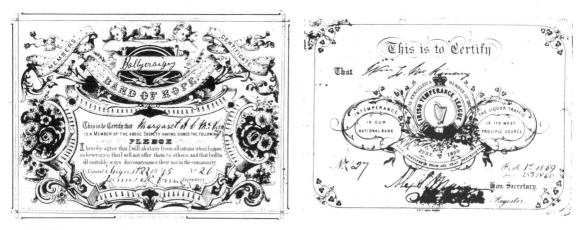

Temperature certificates.

McKinney was closely involved in the setting up and running of the Carnmoney Temperance Society which was established on 1 January 1855. The society's main job was the issuing of cards which pledged the signer to temperance. During McKinney's time as secretary (from December 1858 to March 1860) about 500 people signed up. How long the society lasted is not clear although it seems to have been active until the 1870s. By this time other temperance organisations such as the Band of Hope movement and the Irish Temperance League were active in the local community. In 1867 he was responsible for a local petition which was sent to the government, urging the closing of public houses on Sunday.

He was a member of the board of the Ballycraigy national school. This was run by a board nominated by the Presbyterian church at Carnmoney, but was part of the national school system which by the second half of the

Charabanc outing of Belfast Naturalists' Field Club to Rosapenna, July 1903. William McKinney is seated at the end of the vehicle on the right-hand side.

The exact location of this photograph is not known but it was probably taken on an outing of the Belfast Naturalist Field Club. William McKinney, armed with camera, is on the right.

nineteenth century effectively covered all parts of the country. W.O. McGaw, writing in the 1860s, contrasted the situation with that of fifty years earlier:

Then there were but three schools within the bounds of the parish, and some of these no better than hedge schools. Now there are seven spacious and well-finished buildings set apart from the education of the youth, presided over by well-educated and efficient teachers, and supplied with excellent books and every facility for acquiring information, within the same bounds, and three more immediately in our neighbourhood.

He also commented on the spread of newspapers, in itself an indication of the spread of literacy:

Then the only newspapers published in Belfast were the *Belfast Newsletter*, by Alexander Mackay; and the *Belfast Commercial Chronicle*, by Drummond Anderson: the former was issued twice a week, the latter three times; and neither was half the size of the present *Newsletter*, yet the price was fourpence each. *The Irishman*, by John Lawless, and *The Northern Whig*, by T. D. Finlay, had not then made their appearance.

By the 1860s there were several daily newspapers printed in Belfast, and also weeklies such as the Presbyterian journal, *The Witness*.

By the late 1880s McKinney's interests had extended. As a natural outcome of his interest in antiquities and local history, he became a keen

Members of the Dundee family outside the family home at Hillmount, Carnmoney, 1896 (W.McK.): *standing:* Isaac and his wife Janet (William McKinney's daughter); *seated:* Isabel Kell, John Dundee (died of TB, 1897) and their mother Eliza.

member of the Belfast Naturalist Field Club, along with other friends and relatives such as F.J. Biggar. McKinney went on a lot of their excursions, and it was through these outings that he became friendly with the well-known photographer, R.J. Welch, which may well explain the great interest he was now to take in photography. He acquired a quarter-plate camera and by the early 1890s he was busy photographing not only his friends and family at Sentry Hill but people working on the farm and also his neighbours and their homes. William developed all his own prints from

Mrs Lyle's house in Ballyvesey, not
far from Sentry Hill, 1905
(W.McK.). The child in the pram
outside is her niece.

The Querns occupied this cottage in
Ballycraigy, a short distance from
the back entrance to Sentry Hill.
The Rev. David Quern, seated
directly in front of the doorway,
was a retired Congregationalist
minister; his son David is standing
behind him. David was also a
Congregationalist minister who
went to work in the foreign
missions after serving in the local
church for a time.

Mary Ann Guthrie, King's Moss, 1908 (W.McK.). She was a niece of the Guthrie brothers and worked as a dressmaker from her home.

Miss Ramsay and Mrs Rogers at John Straghan's house, c.1905 (W.McK.). It looks as if neither was that keen on having her photograph taken!

glass negatives; the morning-room could be converted into a darkroom. His photographs are for us today an almost unique portrait of an Irish rural community at the turn of the century.

Joshua Wells, journeyman tailor, c.1895 (W.McK.).

64

Left: Miss Ferguson outside her cottage, close to the back entrance of Sentry Hill, *c.*1900 (W.McK.). Her family had at one time owned the land between Sentry Hill and Sunnyside. The McMillan family eventually acquired the Ferguson land, but as the farm dwelling was in a ruined state they lived at their public house, the Halfway House (now the Chimney Corner), *below left*, with the McMillans in front, *c.*1900 (W.McK.).

As far as social relations were concerned it is clear that William's first rank of associates was his relatives. The Giffins, McGaws and Biggars were frequent visitors at Sentry Hill as were the other families who married into this close circle: the McMordies, Archbolds, Smiths, and later, the Dundees. William did, however, have various friends who visited regularly. One of these was Fergus Wilson, a distant relative, who owned the Blackstaff textile mills – his visits stopped eventually, according to Joe Dundee, because he whistled too much! Most of his close friends belonged to the local Presbyterian group. The minister often called. In the early 1900s the Church of Ireland rector became a close acquaintance of the family, perhaps because of the historical interests he shared with William.

Relations with his immediate neighbours were more functional than familiar. Neighbours helped each other at harvest time, a practice which still continued well into the twentieth century, although already on the decline in the 1880s and 1890s. Sometimes they would borrow equipment from them – for example, Thos. Mullan lent William his fanners to clean corn in the winter of 1861. Neighbours did come together for certain other things. A couple of times in the 1870s people met to discuss the payment of cess which had been increased because of fires in the area. McKinney was involved on a number of occasions as trustee for the wills of neighbours. Rows could break out however. In 1872, for example, McKinney brought Thomas Mullan to court over blasts from his adjacent quarry but it was settled just before the case opened. Another action over water drainage did go to court and Mullan was ordered to pay damages.

Sometimes from McKinney's papers we pick up pieces of scandal and information. In a letter of 1856 from Jane McKinney to J. A. McKinney, she comments:

> John Hill has given poor Katy a severe thrashing, the neighbours went in and saved her and advised her to go home to her friends, but she said she dare not, for, he said she was his property and would punish them if they would harbour her. He has hardly been sober since they went to town, and now is coming back . . .

On another occasion in 1852 McKinney remarks in his diary that a woman in the neighbourhood 'had a young son this morning, which is considered very remarkable as her husband is nearly three years dead and has had 13 children before this one'.

A rather scurrilous tale about a neighbour in Ballycraigy is copied down in one of McKinney's notebooks. Whether or not it pertains to a true story we do not know but according to a reference in the book it was written by one Annie McWilliams (1866–93)

The Buck's Wedding

> *On a farm in Ballycraigy*
> *There lives a famous man,*
> *Who took a notion to get wed,*
> *So he went to Carr's clan.*

AS LARRY SEES THEM.

Newspaper caricature of William Mullan, the only JP in the townland, c.1914. Son of Thomas Mullan, he lived at Rockmount, next door to Fairymount. The Mullans were the only Catholic family in Ballyvesey.

He first commenced with Lydia,
Then tried wee Lizzie too,
But when his han' he ran o'er Ann,
He said 'faith she'll just do'.

He courted her for seven months,
Like a young buckson beau,
And at last big Ann consented,
With the old Buck to go.

The Old Buck is not scarce of mates,
He has three to supply,
But Sarah Gawn is growing old,
And so a fourth he'll try.

He says he wants another heir,
That can eat pork and gravey;
And not a donces puney whelp
Like little Jennie's Davey.

He says Big Ann is beautiful
And strong, and young and fair;
And that she will beat old Mina,
At raising him an heir.

Ann's mother says, 'he's a big match,
His character is grand,
He has twelve cows, and one wee bull,
Besides five farms of land.'

War was declared in the Buck's house,
I heard the neighbours say:
Ann would not go to the bed room
Till the three went away.

Then after the Buck sware awhile,
The three went to the loft,
And left the room to him and Ann,
Where they so oft' had doffed.

Ann is now filled with love and joy,
In her new married state,
And kisses the Buck lovingly,
'Thou he is sixty eight.

Now to conclude my curious tale,
I think these stirring times,
Such weddings, are a mystery
That should be wrote in rhymes.

Next time I write I'll let you know
Of the Old Buck's well-being,
And how his two old concubines
Are with Big Ann agreeing.

Dec. 30, 1889

As regards politics, it is obvious that by William McKinney's time the republican and revolutionary ideas of 1798 had died out in the area. The fighting and the massacres in the south that year had alarmed many; more importantly there were no longer such important causes of protest. The Ordnance Survey Memoir of the 1830s recorded that the people in the district had no interest in politics, apart from some previous unrest over the tithe question which had been largely solved with the arrival of a conciliatory rector.

In the 1850s McKinney records how he and his father attended dinners given by and for Col. T.H. Pakenham, Conservative MP for the county and brother of the landlord of their Mallusk farm. At the 1869 by-election for the county, however, both gave assistance to and voted for the Liberal candidate, and continued to do so at subsequent elections. Concern over the land question was undoubtedly the main cause of their support for the Liberals but religious influence may also have been at work here. After the parliamentary election in Antrim on 12 February 1874, William McKinney writes: 'I voted for Charles Wilson [Liberal]. A great number of Presbyterians are voting for O'Neill and Chance [Conservative], the Episcopalian landlords.' The Liberal candidates in 1880 were also Presbyterians. Most landlords were Church of Ireland and amongst Presbyterians there was a feeling that members of the established church had too strong a position in society: McKinney's newspaper cuttings include letters complaining about how few Presbyterians were magistrates. Also, the Presbyterians were increasingly used to running organisations and societies, an experience which is likely to have made them want a say in society as a whole and so they came to question the role, social and political, of the landlords. The Liberal candidates in Antrim in the general elections of 1874 and 1880 received a very sizeable vote from the Presbyterian tenant farmers of the county, although, thanks to a large, mainly Conservative Belfast section among the voters of the county, they failed to win any seats until the Liberal W.P. Sinclair won a by-election in 1885.

East Antrim Election, 1885.

Mr. DALWAY desires, and, indeed, is most anxious, that every Elector should Vote precisely as his conscience dictates, and he wishes to assure one and all that they can now do so without fear of consequences at the hands of Landlords, Agents, or any other Person whatever, as the Voting by Ballot is **absolutely Secret.**

Please come Early to the Poll.

Polling commences at EIGHT o'Clock, a.m., and closes at EIGHT o'Clock, p.m.

Election notice from the Liberal candidate, M.R. Dalway, 1885.

Polling on FRIDAY, 4th December, 1885.

That same year the Roughfort Liberal Association was formed with William McKinney as secretary. Their aims were fairly general – the equalisation of all religious denominations, the maintenance of peace at home and abroad, and beneficial legislation for all. In the general election of 1885, however, the Liberals were defeated in Antrim and elsewhere in Ulster by the Conservatives. As party organisers in Belfast had emphasised to McKinney in the election run-up, the key to the election in Antrim was the new class of recently enfranchised labourers. The Liberals, with their largely tenant-farmer support, were unable or unwilling to attract them and so lost to the Conservatives who with their strong Orange and gentry element were now able to control the new Unionist organisations which were formed in 1885–6 to face the nationalist threat.

McKinney attended the Ulster Liberal Convention of 19 March 1886 at which the vast majority came out against any scheme to give home rule to Ireland. In the same month he forwarded to 10 Downing Street the resolutions of the Roughfort Liberal Association on the question. These

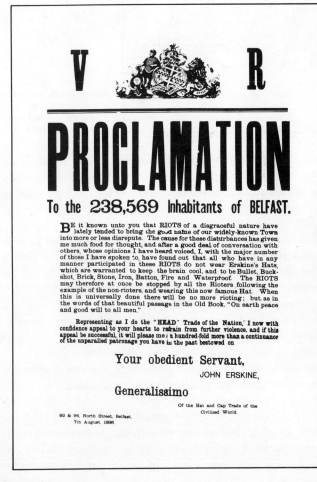

Poster about 1886 Belfast riots. This should be read carefully as it is not quite what it seems!

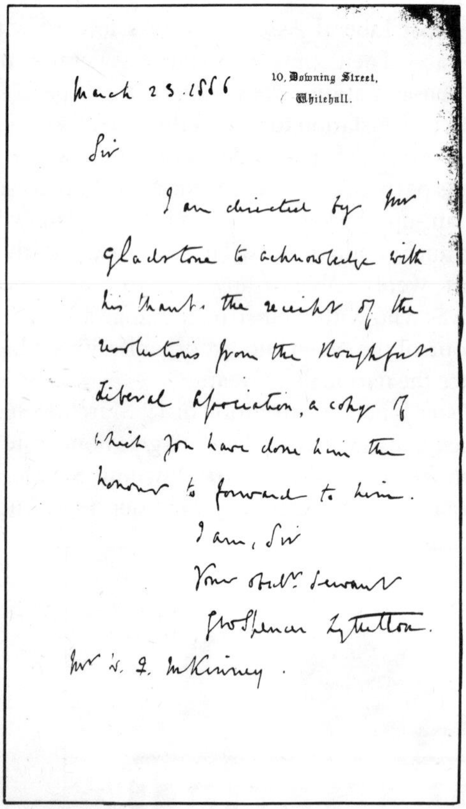

10, Downing Street,
Whitehall.

March 25.1886

Sir

I am directed by Mr
Gladstone to acknowledge with
his thanks the receipt of the
resolutions from the Roughfort
Liberal Association, a copy of
which you have done him the
honour to forward to him.

I am, Sir

Your obd'. servant

[signature] Lyttelton.

Mr W. J. McKinney.

Letter from 10 Downing Street to
William McKinney at Sentry Hill,
acknowledging receipt of the
Roughfort Liberal Association
resolutions, 1886.

declared loyalty to the Crown and opposition to any act likely to lead to
the disintegration of the Empire. They called for provincial boards to deal
with local affairs and suggested a solution to the land question, whereby
tenants would be able to purchase their lands at moderate yearly
instalments.

Hereafter William McKinney played little active part in politics, probably because the Liberal Presbyterian tenant farmers had only a token
place in the new Unionist party structures. The family were still interested
in local issues, however: in 1893–4, while he was living in Belfast, William
served as a member of the Belfast Board of Poor Law Guardians, and from
the early 1900s to his death in the 1930s his son John was a member of the
Belfast Rural Districts Council. In 1912 William signed the Ulster Covenant, pledging his opposition to home rule in Ireland.

Why did the McKinneys become Unionists, and not Nationalists? The
answer lies in their experience of life in nineteenth-century Ireland. Thanks
to the prosperity resulting from industrialisation and the so-called 'Ulster
Custom' which gave tenant farmers certain rights to their land, the major
causes of the growing disillusionment with the Union elsewhere in Ireland
(the Famine, the land question and general economic decline) were not
relevant to most of the people of Carnmoney and indeed much of Ulster.

Besides all this, Nationalism had become identified with Catholicism for various reasons, not least because the people worst effected by the failings of the Union were the Catholics of the south and west of the country. The Nationalists also represented Catholic interests in certain contentious issues such as education, and the prominent part given to the Catholic clergy in the new Nationalist organisations of 1885 was an indication of the close relationship between Church and Party. Joe Biggar, a cousin of the McKinneys, was elected as a home rule MP for Cavan in 1874, and three years later converted to Catholicism, which he saw as 'the national religion'. Certainly by the late 1880s it was generally assumed that Catholics were automatically Nationalists, and Protestants, Unionists.

Quoted by F. Healey in 'J.G. Biggar', *Clio*, 1969, p.12.

None of the McKinneys were members of the Orange Order and references to Orangemen in William's diaries in the 1860s and 1870s were not complimentary. During the Antrim by-election of 1869 he mentions the presence of a 'mean Orange mob'. As a farmer and a Liberal Presbyterian he would not have had much in common with the Order's strongly Conservative working-class Church of Ireland membership. As the Order expanded in the 1880s, however, it gained an important say in the new Unionist organisations, which by the turn of the century had united Protestants of different denominations.

Copy of the Ulster Solemn League and Covenant, signed by William McKinney.

So far our interest in William McKinney has been mainly for the period up to the early 1890s. This is because, with the exception of some years at the end of his life, none of his diaries have survived after this time. But this later stage of McKinney's life must be given some attention. By the 1890s he had ceased to work on the farm which was now run by his son John who, after his marriage in 1890, moved to neighbouring Sunnyside, which he purchased three years later. So by the last decade of the nineteenth century the McKinneys owned three farmhouses and 92 acres. One of their labourers Alic McIlwaine and his family was living at Fairymount.

McKinney maintained and developed his interests. The raising of funds for a new lecture hall for the church occasioned various concerts, fairs and sales of work at Carnmoney, in which he was involved, during the years 1891–4. The highlight of these events was a 'Grand Bazaar and Fancy Fair', held in the church grounds, from 26 to 29 May 1893. A book of the bazaar was produced which gave a history of the area and the church, and listed all the attractions. It was opened by Viscountess Templeton and included work tables, a flower stall, a shooting gallery, an 'antiquarian room' run by McKinney himself, and various other attractions, as well as a full programme of music.

These events were celebrated in a poetic correspondence between William McKinney and his friend Thomas Houston.

A merry Xmas to you Tom,
May blessings on you pour,
And may you end in peace and love
This, eighteen ninety four.

May all your Halls be furnished,
And all your History found,
And all your wants be satisfied,
And nought but joy abound.

Then raise your voice aloud and sing,
And on your neighbours call,
And shout aloud ''Tis finished now,
Our own Great Lecture Hall!'

The Building's up, the Builder's paid,
Then let us all rejoice,
And at the opening service meet,
To sing with cheerful voice.

W. F. McKinney
December 24, 1894

Dear Mr Mc I thank you much
For pretty Xmas poem
Bespattering with flattery
Houston, Thomas, (Tom)

But though the butter's thick laid on
I know it's kindly meant
I therefore gratefully accept
Aware of good intent

But then apart from rosy tints
Are many wishes kind
Which I with thought reciprocal
Am wishing in my mind

I wish that still your shadow may
A burly frame be taken
And may your antiquarian fame
In circles high be spoken.

Thomas Houston
December 28, 1894

By the turn of the century, McKinney had come to be regarded as an important source of information on the history of the area. He assisted a number of writers, including F.J. Biggar, the antiquarian, W. T. Latimer, the Presbyterian historian and D.J. O'Donoghue, author of *Poets of Ireland*. He also wrote to several individuals about the local dialect. Unfortunately we no longer have any of this material on dialect but in one of his notebooks there is a piece on Scottish dialect which would have been largely true for the area. An extract is given here:

Scotch Words

They speak in riddles north beyond the Tweed,
The plain, pure English they can deftly read;
Yet when without the book they come to speak,
Their lingo seems half English and half Greek.

Their jaws are chafts; *their hands, when closed, are* neives;
Their bread's not cut in slices, but in sheives;
Their armpits are their oxters; *palms are* luifs;
Their men are chields; *their timid fools are* cuiffs;
Their lads are callants, *and their women* kimmers;
Good lasses denty queens, *and bad ones* limmers.
They thole *when they endure,* scart *when they scratch;*
And when they give a sample it's a swatch.
Scolding is flytin', *and a long palaver*
Is nothing but a blether *or a* haver.

He became involved in the Linen Hall Library in Belfast and on a number of occasions donated rare early Belfast printed books to the library's collection. In respect of this he was made an honorary member – a rare distinction. Outings with the Belfast Naturalist Field Club remained a popular occurrence for McKinney.

His job as secretary to the Presbyterian congregation still involved him in considerable work. Changes in the church in this later period included moves towards the introduction of instrumental music in the services and the abolition of family pews. Neither finally occurred until after McKinney's time: he was in favour of the first change but was decidedly against the second. Among the papers at Sentry Hill are some documents relating to two ventures in which F.J. Biggar was a leading force. The first was the series of annual Feiseanna held in the Glens of Antrim in the early years of the twentieth century to promote the Gaelic language and culture. The second was the Ulster Public Houses Trust Co., which was an attempt to introduce a new element into the drink business. Whether or not McKinney had any part in these is not clear although we can note that he sold Biggar the land to build a public house, the 'Crown and Shamrock' – the name symbolising a union of British and Irish cultures.

Apart from a brief period, 1893–4, when he rented a house on the Antrim Road, called Throne Villa, McKinney spent the rest of his days at Sentry Hill. After the marriage of his daughter Janet to the local doctor,

ULSTER PUBLIC HOUSES TRUST COMPANY, LIMITED.

Mermaid of Mahee, Inn Sign, Kircubbin.

Templetown Arms, Templepatrick, Co. Antrim.

Seal of the Company.

Crown and Shamrock Inn, Carnmoney, Co. Antrim.

Refreshment Room, Templetown Arms, Templepatrick.

To provide Food and Refreshments of the best kind and in the right way.

No private gain.

Established for the public good by The Ulster Public Houses Trust Co., Limited.

Suggestions may be made to the Secretary, 109 Royal Avenue, Belfast.

Dunleath Arms, Ballywalter, Co. Down.

Isaac Dundee, only one child remained at home, Meg. But he now had the company of his son's children, Elsie and Tom, at Sunnyside. After John's wife died, he and the two children came to live at Sentry Hill. Tom went to RBAI and then attended an agricultural college in Co. Cavan. When he returned to Sentry Hill in 1912, he took over the running of the farm from his father.

While our written evidence for this period is not so full as for the earlier years, we do have valuable oral evidence from his grandchildren and above all, his photographs. From both sources the picture of Sentry Hill which emerges is a happy one with friends and family frequently visiting. The Dundee grandchildren were often at the farm and all today remember this time and their grandfather with great affection.

There were frequent parties at Sentry Hill, and the piano was an

Brochure for F.J. Biggar's Ulster Public Houses Trust Company.

essential source of enjoyment. McKinney continued to photograph his friends and neighbours, and to build up his collection of Irish antiquities and strange objects from abroad. A room at Sentry Hill was turned into a museum. He remained keenly interested in geology and astronomy.

By this stage McKinney spent a lot of time working at another interest of his, genealogy. He had rescued the baptismal, marriage and burial records of Carnmoney Presbyterian congregation from being destroyed. From these he painstakingly constructed family histories for most of the families in the area. This became known as the 'Carnmoney stud book' and for contemporaries of McKinney as well as people today it is an important record of families in the district. It is also a valuable aid to historians.

On 19 September 1905 all the Presbyterian congregation came together in the lecture hall at Carnmoney for a special event in William's honour. After tea, speeches were made in tribute to him. His work for the church and the community was highly praised, how he had preserved the congregational records and had taken note of events and occurrences in the parish; now he was recognised 'as the most reliable authority in connection with the history of the district'. He was then presented with a beautiful illuminated address in album form and a portrait of himself by W.G. MacKenzie.

Thus between William McKinney's birth in 1832 and the outbreak of war in 1914, life at Sentry Hill and the surrounding countryside was transformed. The family prospered and their home was rebuilt several times. Social and religious attitudes had changed from those seen and recorded by the writer of the Ordnance Survey Memoir in the 1830s. New political opinions had emerged by the 1880s and a special cultural and historical view of the world had been formed, all at a period when the mass of people were being educated and enfranchised for the first time. The experiences of the McKinneys give an invaluable insight into the changes which occurred in the character of the Ulster Presbyterian community and which were to prove of lasting importance.

Address to William McKinney on the occasion of the special presentation to him by the Presbyterian congregation on 19 September 1905.

During the early years of the new century parties were often held at Sentry Hill. The photograph below was taken by William McKinney on one such occasion in June 1902. Present were members of all the leading Carnmoney families. They included substantial farming families such as the Chisolms and the Houstons and also those like the McBrides, Wilsons and Boyds who owned local industries.

CARNMONEY PRESBYTERIAN CHURCH.

—————

Address and presentation to
MR. W. F. McKINNEY.

—————

DEAR MR. McKINNEY -- As it is now 50 years since you accepted the Secretary ship of the Congregation, we consider the time an opportune one for giving expression to the very general desire which exists amongst us to mark our appreciation of your disinterested labours in that office, and of the very efficient manner in which you have discharged the duties pertaining to it. During this lengthened period you have not only kept the Congregational minutes and accounts with marvellous neatness and accuracy, but you have, in addition, taken a note of every event of importance which has occurred in the neighbourhood, so that you are now recognised as the most reliable authority in connection with the history of the district.

Our Congregational records, which now exist for a period of 219 years, have been preserved by you with the utmost sacredness and care, and from these you have been always ready to give information to inquiring friends at home or in other lands regarding their ancestors.

We are also very pleased to think that one of our number has, without any special opportunities, been so distinguished as you have been in antiquarian research, the large number of rare and valuable books and relics which you have been able to collect bearing evidence of your genius and industry in this direction.

Like your honoured father, who for over 40 years discharged most faithfully and efficiently the duties of the Eldership, particularly towards the poor and the children of the Sabbath School, so you, in a different department of Church work, have a long and honourable record; and as a token of our appreciation of your Christian character and service to the congregation we ask your acceptance of this Address and an Oil Painting of yourself, and we trust you may yet enjoy many years of health to continue your labour of love in our midst.

(Signed on behalf of the Congregation--
HUGH WATERWORTH, Minister
Wm. RODGERS, Session Clerk.
THOMAS A. ARCHBOLD,
Treasurer.

William McKinney with parrot,
c.1908.

4
'God speed the plough'

So my jolly boys now,
Here's 'God speed the plough',
Long life and success to the farmer.
(Anon., from a McKinney notebook.)

At the centre of life at Sentry Hill was the farm. In the course of William
Fee McKinney's lifetime the state of agriculture at Sentry Hill underwent
dramatic change. This development was partly a result of national trends
such as the growth in prosperity after the Famine, and of the rapid
expansion of Belfast and the consequent demand for food from neighbouring areas such as Carnmoney. Equally important, however, were the
efforts of the McKinneys who 'wrought hard' in the fields.

The writer of the Ordnance Survey Memoir had noted the general
uncultivated state of the farms at Carnmoney in the 1830s. But already, as
his account books for 1830–1 show, Thomas George McKinney was busy
working on his land, digging drains and ditches, and planting hedges. He
improved his fields at Mallusk year after year, lifting large quantities of
boulders and making fences, drains and roads from them. His son,
William, was often involved in this type of work:

> Mon. 1st. March '69. Sam & I wrought in the shough [ditch] at the foot of the
> crossland until 3 o'c when we quit on acct of the rain.

> Tues. 2nd. S & I wrought at the foot of the crossland. I cut the hedge, raised the
> pipe at the big thorn, commenced to put stones in the drain or shoughs.

> Wed. 3rd. Put the last stack into the barn. Eliza went over to my father's. Sam
> and I wrought at the drain filling stones into it. I went up to the school to
> complain of boys annoying John on the road.

During more improvements five years later an accident occurred:

> Mon. 16 March '74. T. McClurg and I took up the two horses to slipe down the
> thorns from the far hill. The old white horse reared up on his hind legs and fell
> over on the top of my leg and hurt the knee. Brought down two loads of the
> thorns and wailed and weighed a load of potatoes. Sent to Carnmoney for three
> leeches to bleed my knee.

As these extracts also show, every field had a name. As well as the
Crossland and the Far Hill there were the Pea Hill, the East and the West
Fauld, the Stack Garden Field and many others.

The farm buildings were constantly maintained and where necessary
rebuilt. Between the 1830s and the 1880s the outhouses and barns were
remodelled to make them as efficient as possible. There was also more

Samuel Black, carpenter and
handyman, who frequently
helped out at Sentry Hill,
c.1895 (W.McK.).

specialised work to be done, such as repairing harness and slaughtering
pigs, for which outside craftsmen or workers were brought in. This poetic
rendering of a bill given to William McKinney, around 1879, by Samuel
Black, a carpenter and local handyman, gives some idea of the range of
work involved.

Account

From Samuel Black of Sandy Knowe,
To Mr Mac with the bald pow,
  This small account I send;
Still trusting that you always may
Have plenty your accounts to pay,
  And something left to spend.

I wrought for near six weeks to you,
And tho a templar good and true,
  My works I did not puff.
When this my small account you've seen,
Which is but two pounds seventeen,
  You'll say it's not enough.

81

According to promise, I send my account,
And I trust that you will not dispute the amount,
For my shoulders and arms got a terrible straining,
With so many weeks of hard sawing, and plaining.

Then dressing and fitting the spokes in the naves,
Is a job that would tire the patience of slaves,
And making the felloes and driving them tight,
Was a job I consider, was done, and done right.

Then for boreing, and straighting, and squaring and driving,
I'll yield to no man in the art of contriving,
For few are my equals, and fewer excel,
And whatever I do, I still like to do well.

Now you have a cart from the shafts to the shears,
That if well housed and painted, may last twenty years,
Its joints are all tight, and its wood is all sound,
And another cart like it, could scarcely be found.

As soon as convenient oblige me and call,
At my office and pay this account which is small,
Bring your purse, which I hope will never feel slack,
And pay like a man, your good friend –
                                    Samuel Black.

Farming required equipment. As the century went on, more specialised and expensive farm implements and machinery were obtained. The purchase of stock was another constant expense for the farmer. When William McKinney acquired Fairymount with its 30 acres in 1861, he paid an additional £200 for stock, crop and implements. A poem in one of his notebooks, possibly by himself, describes a forthcoming auction of farm goods and provides us with a valuable list of the contents of a similar holding.

Saturday, January 12, 1884

Auction Sale, on Saturday,
  At Ballyduff in Carnmoney;
Important auction of live stock,
The remains of Giffens' flock.
Crop, Implements for farming too;
Jaunting car, and Harness new.

Mr S. G. McIlwaine
Does wish no longer to retain
The stock and crop, for he has sold
His uncle's farm, and got the gold.

He therefore offers, without fail
The following list of things for sale,
On January 12 at eleven o'clock
He will offer the following stock –

Tom Montgomery, carpenter,
c.1895 (W.McK.).

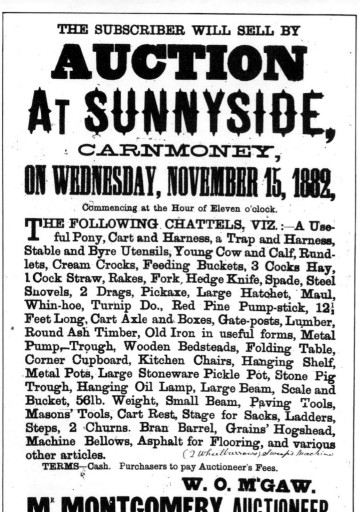

THE SUBSCRIBER WILL SELL BY

AUCTION
AT SUNNYSIDE,
CARNMONEY,
ON WEDNESDAY, NOVEMBER 15, 1882,

Commencing at the Hour of Eleven o'clock.

THE FOLLOWING CHATTELS, VIZ.:—A Useful Pony, Cart and Harness, a Trap and Harness, Stable and Byre Utensils, Young Cow and Calf, Rundlets, Cream Crocks, Feeding Buckets, 3 Cocks Hay, 1 Cock Straw, Rakes, Fork, Hedge Knife, Spade, Steel Shovels, 2 Drags, Pickaxe, Large Hatchet, Maul, Whin-hoe, Turnip Do., Red Pine Pump-stick, 12½ Feet Long, Cart Axle and Boxes, Gate-posts, Lumber, Round Ash Timber, Old Iron in useful forms, Metal Pump—Trough, Wooden Bedsteads, Folding Table, Corner Cupboard, Kitchen Chairs, Hanging Shelf, Metal Pots, Large Stoneware Pickle Pot, Stone Pig Trough, Hanging Oil Lamp, Large Beam, Scale and Bucket, 56lb. Weight, Small Beam, Paving Tools, Masons' Tools, Cart Rest, Stage for Sacks, Ladders, Steps, 2 Churns, Bran Barrel, Grains' Hogshead, Machine Bellows, Asphalt for Flooring, and various other articles. *(2 Wheelbarrows) Sweep's Machine*

TERMS—Cash. Purchasers to pay Auctioneer's Fees.

W. O. M'GAW.
M. MONTGOMERY, AUCTIONEER.

Sunnyside, October 23rd, 1882.   J. Reed, Printer, Victoria Street, Belfast.

Three farm horses, and ten milch cows,
Two yearling calves, and two broad sows,
Three pokes of meadow hay he'll sell,
And twenty stacks of oats as well.

And any one who turnips needs,
Can get an acre of prime swedes.
Mower and reaper too, combined,
Plough, Grubber, and harrows, well tined.

One turnip pulper, almost new,
Two farm carts, and cart harness too.
A famous Irish jaunting car,
With splendid harness by O'Hayer.

Dairy utensils, none made better,
Kitchen furniture &c.
Terms Cash with 5 Commission,
To Samson Clark, man of precision.

Sam Williamson, thatcher, at
Fairymount, *c*.1895 (W.McK.).

The papers at Sentry Hill contain
many brochures for farming
equipment, similar to this one for a
'twine self-binding harvester'.

The rise in prosperity of the McKinneys over this whole period is well indicated by the way in which their land holdings increased. On his marriage in 1831, Thomas George McKinney held a perpetuity lease for 33 statute acres at Sentry Hill, plus another 12 statute acres, adjacent in Mallusk. Ten years later he acquired a lease on a further 32 acres in Ballyvesey though these were sold in 1865. In 1861 William McKinney purchased the lease for Fairmount and its 31 acres. Finally, the addition of Sunnyside meant that a further 16 acres had been added to the family holding. All this land, except for the Mallusk farm, was held in perpetuity leases; in other words the leases were renewable for ever.

Dairy farming was the principal feature of the agricultural scene around Sentry Hill, due to the demand from Belfast for fresh milk products. From T.G. McKinney's accounts in the early 1830s we know he made regular sales of butter and buttermilk to Belfast. William occasionally helped him with this, and when he ran his own farm at Fairymount he made very frequent trips to Belfast. Containers known as rundlets were used for carrying buttermilk (the diaries and account books refer simply to milk but

Work in progress on a new hay shed, 1903 (W.McK.). This shed was erected by the Belfast firm of Potts & Houston. The bill came to £52.

86

Tom McIlwaine with a dairy shorthorn cow, *c*.1905 (W.McK.).

this was in fact buttermilk); butter was sold in firkins. Many entries in the diaries relate to aspects of dairying. In May 1850 he records that his father had a horse-driven churning machine installed. In December 1851 he mentions making a wooden chimney for the milk house – where the milk was matured. Some interesting side references are worth noting on this subject of dairying. On 26 May 1859, 'George McMullan had Bell Scott at the petty sessions for milking his cows. She took her child in her arms to squall and fainted when her name was called. Her trial was postponed.' What happened to her finally is not mentioned. We can also read, from the 1850s on, of farmers being brought before Belfast courts for adulteration of milk – a sign of the growing health and quality standards.

It seems that in the 1830s it was usual for the womenfolk in the family to do the milking but by the second half of the century this had changed, perhaps because with their greater prosperity they could afford milk maids. At the same time the churning and the preparation of butter, often done at two or three in the morning, so it would be fresh that day, was supervised by the woman of the house. When William McKinney's wife died, Susan Easton, a former labourer at Sentry Hill, came to help with the churning for a while. By the latter part of the century, however, it was probably not regarded as proper or respectable for a well-to-do farmer's wife to do the actual milking. In the 1890s a friend of William McKinney's, Thomas Houston, wrote an obituary for a farmer's wife, Mrs Martha Carson. This gave great offence to her sisters Ethel and Jane Biggar who stated: 'such a document should never have been printed, and if our feelings had been consulted most assuredly never would'.

The section which probably insulted them most and perhaps disturbed their more refined memories of their sister was the one relating to her household and dairy duties:

In the summer time, it was her custom to rise at three o'clock in the morning to get the churning commenced; and, while this process was going on, she would hurry off to bathe – a mile distant – and be back in time to dress and print the butter, after which she would invariably milk her share, often a third, of thirty cows. Such was her regular morning's work for five days in the week, which being finished, she entered upon her ordinary household duties. Quite frequently she would start on foot in the afternoon to visit her friends, at a distance of four miles, always returning in time for the milking in the evening. At milking she was almost unequalled. On one occasion she visited on his deathbed an old servant, who had acted as cattleman to Mr Carson for a long period. The old man, on being told that Mrs Carson had come to see him, exclaimed: 'Ay weel, mony a time I did say she could milk a coo wae onny woman.'

They may also have taken exception to some of the other comments in Houston's leaflet:

She had a strong nerve and steady hand, a fact exemplified by the way in which she shot a blackbird from her scullery window. She had an antipathy to these birds on account of their fruit-stealing propensities.

Not even the fulsome praise of the conclusion salved their feelings.

Richly adorned with that which becometh women professing godliness – good works – Mrs Carson came to her grave in a full age, as a shock of corn cometh in in his season.

The cows were kept in the fields from around April to the end of September. While housed in winter sheds they were fed meadow hay. 'Slummage', the residue of the grain used in the local distilleries, was sometimes bought. On 30 June 1854 William writes: 'Left home before 3 o'clock and went to the distillery for grains. There were 54 carts before me when I went. I waited until half past six at night and had then to give back my ticket and come home without any.'

The McKinneys do not seem to have owned a bull until the 1880s. There are many references to taking cows to bulls on neighbouring farms – sometimes with little success: on 21 June 1877, for example, 'John took Dandy to Thos Biggar's (3rd time)'.

The cows are occasionally referred to as the 'black moiley' or 'young red heifer', but often they have names such as Ena, Young Beauty and Dora. Prior to the 1870s the tendency seems to have been to sell the calves or kill them for veal and only in the late 1870s do they sell cattle, and even then this was not a major contribution to the family budget. Fairs at Belfast and Templepatrick were the main markets for cattle when they were sold. Entries in the diaries tell of cattle being slaughtered at home and their hides being sold. The McKinneys often did the killing and skinning themselves.

William McKinney attended cattle shows in Belfast, no doubt to see new breeds of cattle, and occasionally other wonders. On 28 June 1865 he records in his diary: 'I went to see the cattle show. There were two Emus at it and a great show of fowls and implements.' In the 1860s the stock at Sentry Hill and Fairymount were mainly moiley cows but by 1914 the majority were dairy shorthorns. It is interesting to note the many references from the 1880s onwards to veterinary surgeons coming to see cows on the farm.

WHAT HE MIGHT HAVE BEEN.

MR. ROBERT BARKLIE.

Instead of being the Public Analyst, he might have been a milkman.

A newspaper caricature (c.1905) of Robert Barklie who was responsible for quality control of Belfast's milk.

Card found in a book at Sentry Hill with a list of female names written on the back.

SHORTHORN BULL

"EMPEROR,"

THE PROPERTY OF WILLIAM SPEERS,

WILL STAND THIS SEASON AT

MOUNTPLEASANT, MONKSTOWN.

COLOUR : DARK RED.

Bred by JOHN MULLHOLLAND, Esq., M.P., Ballywalter Park.

Calved, January 20th, 1876.

			No. in Herd Book.
SIRE—LORD WOODLANDS.	(817. J. H. B.)		
DAM—KATE GWYNNE,	-	by MAXIMUS GWYNNE.	(29347. C H. B.)
G. D.—WHITE KATE,	-	by IRISHMAN.	(552. J. H. B.)
G. G. D.—KATE, -	-	by DEFENDER.	(427. J. H. B.)
G. G. G. D.—KATE, -	-	by EMPEROR.	(408. J. H. B.)
G. G. G. G. D.—KATE.	by FALSTAFF,	by WELCOME GUEST.	(15297. C. H. B.)

Terms : 5s.

TO BE PAID AT TIME OF SERVICE.

Hayshed, *c.*1901 (W.McK.). On the right can be seen some of the various carts at Sentry Hill, as well as a roller and a hand drawn slipe for removing large stones from the field.

Horses also played an important part in the everyday activities of the household. For a host of tasks, like ploughing, or carrying people and goods to town, the horses were in daily use and were essential. They might also be used for work outside the farm – in 1849, for instance, William did horsework at the draining work done for the new dam at Cottonmount.

Some verses in one of William's notebooks mention two of the horses:

Our old white horse, his name is Ned,
On straw or rushes he makes his bed
He shakes his tail and tosses his head,
To get his oats in the morning.

Our big horse Billy a good brown bay,
He draws the straw, and draws the hay,
And butter, and buttermilk, far away
To Durham street in the morning.

William's diaries contain a number of references to buying and selling farm horses, as do his father's accounts. On 4 February 1857, for example, Thomas McKinney gave £18 for a horse at the Belfast fair. Amongst the papers at Sentry Hill is a note dated March 1873 about another horse bought in Belfast. Signed with 'his mark', Thomas Hill of Magheramorne states: 'I hereby guarantee the White Horse sold this day in Belfast Fair to do all kinds of work placidly and quietly to the best of his ability.' Let us hope the horse lived up to this guarantee! One which did not is mentioned in a notice from one William Carson to Joseph McGaw of Fairymount, in 1853, saying that the black horse sold in exchange for a cow and calf and one shilling 'refuses to draw and is a restive horse contrary to your said warranty'. He demanded that McGaw should take the horse back or he would auction it and charge him what he lost in the deal.

The horses sometimes required special care. On one occasion in February 1854, William 'walked about all night with the horse that has the lockjaw; took 12 quarts of blood from him'. With two horses at Fairymount and three at Sentry Hill, visits to the blacksmith were common occurrences. The following extracts from a poem composed by William Campbell, an illiterate from Ballyhenry, describe the work of the local smith.

It's upwards now of twenty year
Since Jamey Boyd commenced here
No other smith set up in sight
Which made him work with all his might

When he set up at his own hand
He had but little to command
But Providence to him proved kind
In peace and plenty he does shine

* * *

Alic McIlwaine at work in front of Sentry Hill with two horses and a swing plough. The photographer's grandson, Tom, looks on, 1906 (W.McK.).

I hope the Lord will give him grace
And keep him working in this place
At ploughs and harrows he can't be bate
And shoeing horse both tight and neat

* * *

He has had many an apprentice chiel
And learned them to shoe horses weel
For poverty they need not fear
If they work like what they did when here.

McKinney used Boyd until 1872 but then changed to another blacksmith, apparently because of a quarrel with Boyd. On 30 November 1872 he writes in his diary, 'Jamie Boyd called to borrow money from me. He annoyed W. J. Carlisle and was pushed down on the causeway.'

The horses' harness also needed attention from time to time. In May 1851, for example, Stewart Beggs, a saddler, spent almost two weeks at the house, repairing and making new harnesses.

Trotting matches were sometimes held in the district. Every Christmas day there were horse races. The races on 25 December 1863 were more eventful than usual:

Went to the horse race in James Boyd's fields. Dogherty's horse won the first race and McKeown's the second. A young rider was almost killed. There was some fighting on the platform. James & Wm McKelvey were kick'd off it.

On Christmas day 1889 'John & Hugh went to Dunanney to assist in catching three Yankee horses that have been on the grass for two months'.

Reconstruction of Sentry Hill house and farm, 1900.
Drawn by David Evans, 1981

See how the barn has been built on a slope so that a cart can be conveniently backed to the level of the first floor for loading and unloading.

The house: ground floor plan

1 dining-room
2 store
3 bathroom
4 scullery
5 kitchen
6 pantry
7 morning room
8 drawing room
9 hall and steps to other floors

The outbuildings

10 churn house
11 horse walk to power the churn
12 creamery
13 wash house (with harness room above)
14 store for side cars, with steps up to harness room above.
15 mounting block
16 potato house
17 store for farm carts
18 stables
19 meal store
20 cow byre
21 granary steps
22 granary
23 threshing machine
24 horse walk to power the threshing machine
25 door to granary
26 position of fanner in granary on 1st floor
27 manure heap

Tom Couley, pig killer, c.1900 (W.McK.).

Where these horses came from or what happened to them is not mentioned in the diaries.

In the early period hunting with horses and hounds does not seem to have been a feature of the farming community. By the early 1890s, however, there are references in the diaries to hounds hunting through Ballyvesey and these were probably from the East Antrim Hunt, founded in the 1890s. William McKinney never hunted but his son John was a founder member of the East Antrim Hunt as was Dr Isaac Dundee, Janet McKinney's husband. Prior to this time, the Marquis of Donegall with

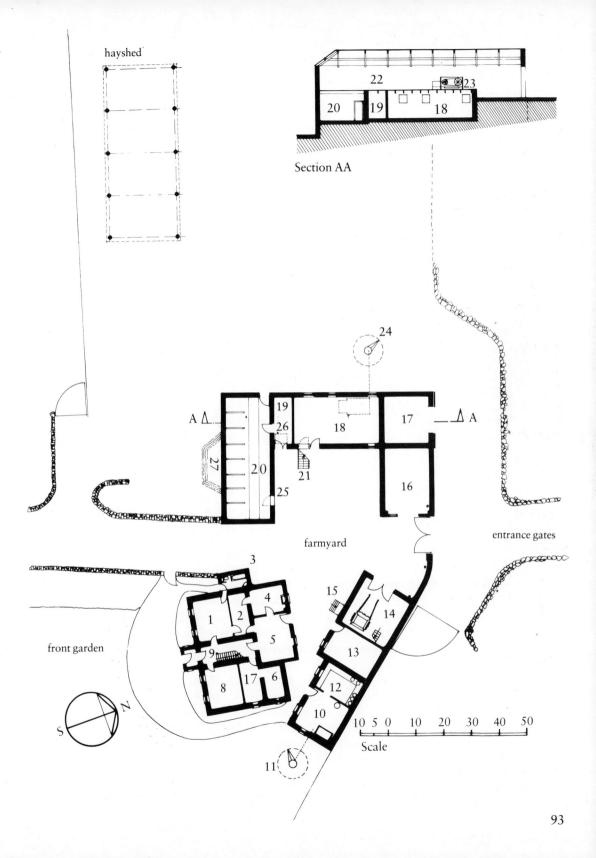

hayshed

Section AA

24

A △ A

farmyard

entrance gates

front garden

3

S N

11

10 5 0 10 20 30 40 50
Scale

other gentry had hunted over the area. The new East Antrim Hunt was composed largely of farmers and local professional men, a sign perhaps of the growth of confidence among this group.

Other animals are referred to in the diaries. Pigs were reared at Sentry Hill although not in great numbers. Pig killers usually visited the farm to slaughter them and dress the carcasses. Hens, ducks, turkeys and geese were reared, mainly for family use. In the late 1880s John McKinney introduced sheep but this experiment was not successful and they were soon removed. There were always dogs, of course. On 3 December 1878 William records that one of his father's dogs 'Donald' died from poison given to it by thieves who stole a horse's collar and some cart wheels from Sentry Hill: the collar was later found in a Belfast pawnbrokers.

Important as dairying increasingly became, tillage remained an essential part of farming. In Ireland as a whole cereal production fell considerably between the famine and 1900, due to an increase in cereal imports, particularly of wheat and barley, from the 1870s onwards. (Oat production also dropped but not so much as the other cereal crops.) This had little effect on Sentry Hill, since the rich light loam there was not suitable for either barley or wheat. This soil is however suitable for oats and other crops such as potatoes and turnips.

Isaac Dundee, on reaping machine, with farm hands and helpers at the corn harvest, c.1904. As well as being the local doctor, Isaac Dundee farmed some forty acres. The boy on the right is making straps with which to bind the stooks of corn.

94

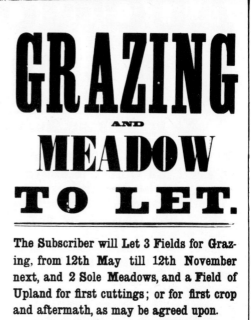

From McKinney's diaries a good picture emerges of the yearly routine of the farmer on the land. During the last two months of the year, grass or lay land was ploughed to break up the soil, but ploughing for seed beds did not begin until February or March. Neighbours often helped, especially in the 1850s when great numbers of people were engaged, but later on only close neighbours or relatives seem to have been present. In March 1851 McKinney records that he joined a party of twenty neighbours to help William Carlisle to plough and plant potatoes and also that George McMullan had eleven people to assist him. The diaries mention cross cutting during ploughing. This was a means of breaking up soil for better seed beds. Ploughing with a long yoking is mentioned by McKinney.

Oats, always called corn, were extensively grown at Sentry Hill. The seed was sown in late March or early April and apart from occasional weeding, the crop was left until September when the oats were mowed with hooks. They were tyed, bound in ten-sheave stooks (set upright to allow drying), made into huts and then put in stacks in the stack-yard. On the 1st September 1873, for example, we read how 'Alex Barkley commenced to sow the corn in the crossland, Margt Crawford lifted. John made straps. Thos held back the corn with a rod. I tyed and stooked. Got 89 stooks cut today.' (John and Thomas were two of McKinney's children.) The corn was eventually threshed and cleaned, when required, before being sold or used at the farm.

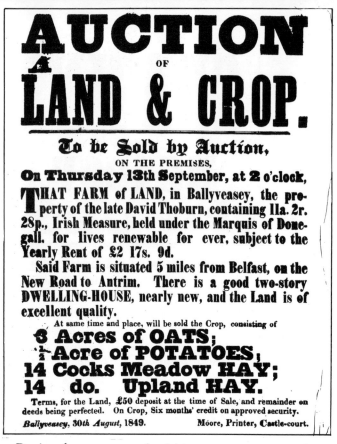

AUCTION

OF

LAND & CROP.

To be Sold by Auction,

ON THE PREMISES,

On Thursday 13th September, at 2 o'clock,

THAT FARM of LAND, in Ballyveasey, the property of the late David Thoburn, containing 11a. 2r. 28p., Irish Measure, held under the Marquis of Donegall. for lives renewable for ever, subject to the Yearly Rent of £2 17s. 9d.

Said Farm is situated 5 miles from Belfast, on the New Road to Antrim. There is a good two-story DWELLING-HOUSE, nearly new, and the Land is of excellent quality.

At same time and place, will be sold the Crop, consisting of

8 Acres of OATS;
½ Acre of POTATOES,
14 Cocks Meadow HAY;
14 do. Upland HAY.

Terms, for the Land, £50 deposit at the time of Sale, and remainder on deeds being perfected. On Crop, Six months' credit on approved security.

Ballyveasey, 30th August, 1849.   Moore, Printer, Castle-court.

During these years much of this process became mechanised. From the diaries we can see that hand flails were used to thresh corn until 1870. In early December of that year William McKinney went to his Uncle John's to observe Sam Blackwell's threshing machine. Later in the same month he bought timber and iron to make a threshing machine and by late 1871 it was in operation in the barn. It was powered by a horse-walk outside the barn.

On 1 January 1876 William records in his diary how the family helped out with the thresher:

> I attended the thrashing machine until dinnertime when we got the slack nearly finished. John attended me. Thos & Joe drove the horse. Sam Biggar tied the straw. Put another stack into the barn which was the last one from the fore hill. Sam Guthrie came here today and made hay mats for the horse's straddle. I drove him home and took two bags of chaff to his house.

While the machine greatly facilitated threshing it did have its dangers. In January 1872, for instance, one of the labourers 'got two fingers burnt with the thrasher'. Another mechanical advance was the combined mowing and binding machine bought from a local firm, McErvil, at the Belfast cattle show, on 20 June 1884. There was a single reaper machine at Sentry Hill before this.

In the early 1850s the McKinneys bought seed oats in Belfast and Larne but by 1855 they were preparing and selling seed oats themselves. They

FARM
TO BE LET.

THE SUBSCRIBERS,

Wishing to Let, for the term of Ten Years (to commence at the First day of November next), all their

FARM IN BALLYVESEY,

PARISH OF CARNMONEY, & COUNTY OF ANTRIM,

Containing Twenty Acres, Irish Plantation Measure, or thereabouts, be the same more or less, will receive written proposals for same, until the 13th of September next.

A Fine of £200 will be required at the First of November, exclusive of the Rent which may be agreed upon.

The House and Offices are in good repair, and the Land is in excellent order.

J. & W. J. M'GAW.

Fairy-Mount, Carnmoney,
Aug. 13th, 1856.

A. WELSH, Printer, 10, Arthur-Square, Belfast.

Potato drills at the front of a local
farmer's house, 1901 (W.McK.).

97

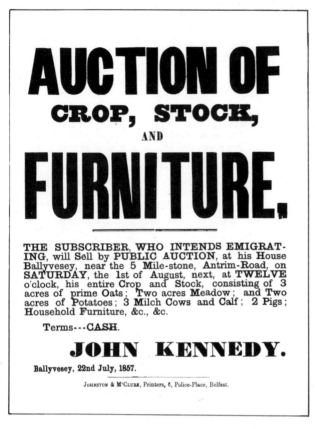

continued to buy new brands of seed to experiment with and William's
diaries contain careful records of which variety was planted in each field
and what quantities of oats were produced. This crop had important
by-products. The worst oats were taken to the mill to be crushed for the
cows. The horses received whole oats. After the oats were riddled the chaff
was emptied into bags which were sold to make mattresses. Straw could be
sold to local brickworks. The McKinneys and their neighbours helped
harvest oats for both the Presbyterian minister and the Congregationalist
minister. In August 1859, sixty people worked on the Rev. Mr Quern's
harvest.

By 1849 the potato crop was beginning to return to normal conditions
in the Carnmoney area after the diseases of the famine period. Because the
potato was only one of a number of crops in the district, its failure had had
no serious effect. As a sign of the bad times, nonetheless, we can note an
entry in McKinney's diary on 30 January 1849 that thieves stole great
quantities of oats and potatoes from farms in the Ballyvesey neighbourhood. By 1851, however, potatoes were again a major crop at Sentry
Hill. On 4 June McKinney records: 'my father had 10 men digging and
shovelling in the furrows on Orr's Hill.'

The potatoes were set in drills about March or April. In June the drills
were grubbed and moulded. Grubbing meant a horse pulling a saddle
harrow, shaped like the drills, to clear weeds off the surface of the soil. The

soil then had to be 'moulded' (replaced back on top of the drills). In October and November the potatoes were lifted and wailed (sorted into different sizes and qualities), before being put into a potato pit. The pit was formed by placing a load of straw on a dry part of the soil, putting potatoes on it and throwing soil over them. The soil had to be carefully shaped to let rainwater escape. The pits were then thatched and topped, to keep the potatoes free from frost. All these processes are well documented in McKinney's diaries.

In 1864, for example, an entry for 25 April notes:

Davy Hunter came from my father's work and commenced at 9 o'c to assist Sam and set in the low field and set every day full time until Saturday night. I harrowed, lifted furrows, ribbed and drove out the manure. Susan scaled the manure and dropped the potatoes. We set them all white rock with the exception of 6 or 8 ridges of skerries at the east side. Set 5 ridges per day on Fri. & Sat. on W. side.

Later, in October and November, there are many entries which just say: 'Sam dug and I wailed'. Sometimes they were joined by others. On 5 November it is recorded:

Sam & I both dug today and Wm & Sus[n] gathered and put the diseased ones by themselves as they gather. Commenced to make a pit without wailing the small ones out. About half the field is done.

In the 1870s he records that the children stayed at home from school to help with lifting the potatoes.

Most potatoes raised on Irish farms were for the farmer's own consumption but the proximity of Belfast created extra demand for this crop. In 1852 William McKinney remarked that one of his father's labourers, John Lawther, had carted potatoes to the Belfast market almost every day for three weeks. As with oats, the McKinneys experimented with different types of potato. The diaries carry references to Australian, Champion, Magnum Bonum, California, Rock, Kerry, and Victorian potatoes. At Sentry Hill there is a poem in praise of the 'tatie' on a 1840s ballad broadsheet by Thomas Beggs (1789–1847) who worked as a labourer at a bleachworks near Hydepark at Mallusk, within sight of Sentry Hill.

> Wi' gladsome heart, and blithesome e'e,
> Thou precious root, I gaze on thee;
> To mony a starv'ling wilt thou be
>   A rare delight,
> An' weel I wat thou are to me
>   A welcome sight!
>
> How we ha'e fen'd, nine months an' mair,
> On parritch thin – a scanty share –
> Wad puzzle mony a head o'lear
>   To tell, I trow;
> But thou art there, an' plague may care!
>   We'll a' be fu'.

99

Weel crack'd thou art, an' floury white;
The nicest gab thou might'st invite,
Thou staff an' stay o' mony a wight,
                    Man, wife, an' wean,
Wha lang ha'e borne the bitter bite
                    O' hungry pain.

When placed upon the table board,
Wi' beans an' peas, an ample hoard,
An' butter, by the gudewife stored,
                    An' cabbage-kail,
I wad say grace like ony Lord,
                    For sic a meal.

Swedes and various types of turnips and mangold wurzels were also grown at Sentry Hill. The turnips were mashed with a pulper and used as winter fodder for the cattle. On 25 December 1874 William recorded a great wonder of the farming world around Carnmoney: 'Went to John Campbell's and saw a turnip said to be 26½lbs in weight. I measured it 41 inches by 35 ins. circumference'. Other vegetables were cabbage, carrots,

The cottage at Hydepark where Tom Beggs, writer of this poem on the 'tatie', lived, here photographed in 1896 (W.McK.).

Receipt for flax.

leeks and peas, all mainly for use in the home. Unlike these crops, flax was raised as a cash product. Up to around 1870 this crop increased in importance in the area, especially during the American civil war when the 'cotton famine' caused a linen boom, but thereafter it declined. Even before 1870 it was not a very extensive crop because it required much labour and flax is a soil-exhaustive plant. Rising imports from abroad reduced prices and the acreage given to flax.

At Sentry Hill the flax seed, of the Dutch or Riga variety, was sown in April. Four months later the flax was pulled and brought to the flax dam to ret. There were seven flax dams at Sentry Hill, supplied by water from Carnmoney Bog and Colinward, which were very suitable for retting. In the diaries in early July 1865 we read:

Fri.5 A wet forenoon. 7 of my father's women pulled flax after dinner. Sam got the pony shod.

Sat. 6   The women got done pulling before 11 o'c. J. Lawther, Susan and I put all the flax into the dam at the foot of my father's E. fauld [field]. Sam & George Gourley drove it to us. Got done with it about 6 o'c after holed 3 loads of my father's.

Hay being taken from the field (probably to be sold), September 1902 (W.McK.).

After a time the flax was laid out to dry. On 24 August he records: 'D. Caldwell had the lint out of the hole up Wilson's loanin side before seven o'c. It was spread at Mallusk. He got done before night'. Finally it was cleaned and then sold, either before or after being scutched.

Up to 1865 William McKinney grew flax at Fairymount but from that time on he did not keep it himself as a crop, although he rented out a couple of fields to his brother John to grow it, and he did occasionally assist his father who retained some land at Sentry Hill under flax. In the late 1850s and early 1860s, the McKinneys obtained up to 10s. per stone for flax but by 1883 they were only receiving 6s.9d. per stone.

The hay rake which brought in the hay to be made into a rick, *c*.1905 (W.McK.).

Permanent pasture and hay were very important at Sentry Hill and at Fairymount, to feed the cattle kept there. The grass seed was normally sown along with corn which, as it grew, helped to protect the grass. On 20 March 1862, William recorded that he 'sowed seeds in the W. hill before dinner and clover and grass seed after'. The corn was cut in September and the grass used for a short period for grazing. The following year, cattle grazed in the field or hay was let grow and harvested in July. Scythes were used at Sentry Hill from the 1830s, if not before, and by the 1870s a mowing machine was in operation. Two days after it was cut, the hay was turned and raked into rows. When dry, it was made into ricks which were eventually carried on a slip or rick-shifter and built into much larger 'pikes' in the field or in the stack-yard. The McKinneys also produced grass seed for sale in Belfast.

In 1863, a typical year, William noted that Sam Easton 'commenced to

103

mow' the hay at Fairymount on 21 July; a week later McKinney himself 'lapped' the hay [rolled it in laps to let the air through]. The hay was then ricked, and on 14 August, 'got up at 4 o'c and brought the rick that we left in the meadow and finished the two pikes with it'. Finally, on the last day of August, 'Sam & I thatched and crowned the 3 hay pikes in the stack yard'. This was to keep it dry; often the pike was also surrounded by paling to keep off the cows! Some of the hay was used by the McKinneys for their own animals but the rest was sold profitably, usually in Belfast, where there was great demand, because of the great numbers of horses kept there for transport.

This period saw important scientific advances in farming at Sentry Hill. Crop rotation was normal procedure by the 1830s. It began with the land in pasture. The pattern then was: year 1, oats; year 2, oats; year 3, potatoes and turnips; year 4, oats and grass seed; year 5, hay for grazing, and ending with a year's grazing.

There was increasing use of fertilisers and new machinery. We have

Tom McKinney driving rick shifter, c.1909 (W.McK.) and his aunt Meg, *seated*, with his sister Elsie, *right*, and friend Mary Bird. The rick shifter could be lowered underneath ricks and then pulled up so that the hay could be moved.

already noted that a horse-drawn threshing machine was installed in 1870, and a combine harvester was purchased in 1884. McKinney's diaries and accounts list other pieces of new equipment including an American rake, bought in 1875, and a force pump, acquired in 1875. Wire was used for fencing from 1875, if not before. Lime was being purchased in the 1830s and was obviously extensively used in the fields. In one of many similiar entries in his diaries William writes on 25 July 1882: 'John took the two horses to the Whitewell for lime. He got 14 barrels for 15/8. Put it in lumps on the far hill. Carted up water in rundlets and slacked it.'

As early as 1855 we have a reference to T. G. McKinney obtaining guano for turnips, and by the 1860s other fertilisers included coke (rich in potash) which was brought from Belfast to cover drills of potatoes. Salt screenings were also used to improve the soil. A contemporary advertisement for Shannon & Holden salt from Carrickfergus advocated that

crushed rock salt should be applied in the Autumn to the stubbles, before they are turned over. This not only kills the parasites, but also destroys twitch and other vegetable rubbish, converting them into good manurial agents; thus cleaning the land without the trouble of gathering and burning the roots in the spring.

From the late 1860s there are many references in the diaries to the use of roadstuff on the land. This was road stone dust and was valuable for putting on boggy land to improve the soil texture. Sometimes it was mixed with lime.

The new fertilisers and sprays which became available were well publicised in the leaflets issued by the Department of Agriculture from the last decade of the nineteenth century onwards. However, important as the new fertilisers became, they did not replace animal manure. In McKinney's diaries there are innumerable references to bringing manure back from Belfast after delivering buttermilk or potatoes. A typical entry is that of 10 July 1868:

Went to town with milk and butter. Sam brought home the last 2 loads of the manure under the rundlets. I waited for the auction of manure and bought three yards for my father at 10 shillings per yd. Paid my cess out of my father's Mallusk cess. Came home in the bus.

The auction referred to was the regular sale of manure at the council stables.

The McKinneys obtained manure from various sources such as the stables of *The Belfast Telegraph* and occasionally the barracks of a cavalry regiment. Problems arose in 1878 over this latter source. On 20 April he writes:

John went to the barracks for a load of manure. I will take no more of it as they want 6d per horse instead of 5d. Put manure into drills. Mary Jane dropped the potatoes and I covered them.

At both Sentry Hill and Fairymount there were extensive dunghills. Horse manure, which was very rich in nitrogen, was usually used mixed with cow and hen manure. The manure was then scaled which involved scattering it

OUTRAGE & REWA...

WHEREAS, on the Night of the 8th, or early on the Morning the 9th inst., THREE GATES, the property of Thomas Prince, of Carnmoney Glebe, were Maliciously Broken in Pieces by some person or persons at present unknown,

WE, whose Names are hereunto subscribed, do hereby offer a Reward of

TWENTY POUNDS,

In proportion to the Sums annexed to our respective names, to any person or persons who will prosecute to Conviction, within six calendar months from the date hereof, the perpetrator or perpetrators of said Outrage; or, a Reward of

TEN POUNDS

For such private information as will lead to the detection of all or any of the persons concerned therein, within six calendar months as aforesaid.

Dated this 10th December, 1863.

	£ s d		£ s d		£ s d
Rev. Geo. C. Smyth,	£10 0 0	Samuel Anderson, ...	£2 0 0	William Agnew,	£2 0 0
R. Grimshaw, J.P., D.L.,	10 0 0	Hugh Rodgers, ...	2 0 0	John M'Ilwaine,	2 0 0
Sir E. Coey, Knt., J.P.,	10 0 0	John Smyth, ...	2 0 0	John Hunter, ...	2 0 0
Rev. R. W. Bland, J.P.,	10 0 0	James Blair, ...	2 0 0	Thomas Nesbit, ...	2 0 0
John Thomson, J.P.,	10 0 0	John Smyth, ...	2 0 0	Thomas Stewart, ...	2 0 0
James Thompson, J.P.	10 0 0	Thomas Bigger, ...	2 0 0	James Green, ...	2 0 0
James Gray, ...	10 0 0	Edward Henderson, ...	2 0 0	William Anderson, ...	2 0 0
Hugh M'Calmont,	10 0 0	James Henderson, ...	2 0 0	Samuel Williamson, ...	2 0 0
Joseph Bigger, ...	10 0 0	Thomas Smyth, ...	2 0 0	Clements Bell, ...	2 0 0
James Harper, ...	10 0 0	Alexander M'Connell,	2 0 0	James Barklimore, ...	2 0 0
Henry Campbell & Co.,	10 0 0	John Chisom, ...	2 0 0	James Vint, ...	2 0 0
Thomas Archibold, ...	10 0 0	John Green, ...	2 0 0	William Moreland, ...	2 0 0
Thomas Prince, ...	10 0 0	John Curran, ...	2 0 0	William Orr M'Gaw,	1 10 0
Rev. Joseph Barkley,	5 0 0	Joseph Quiery, ...	2 0 0	Wm. F. M'Kinney, ...	1 10 0
Samuel Giffen, ...	5 0 0	Samuel Barklimore, ...	2 0 0	Margaret Fulton, ...	1 0 0
James Moreland, ...	5 0 0	William Farquhar, ...	2 0 0	Andrew Moreland, ...	1 0 0
John Dundee, M.D., ...	5 0 0	Robert Lewis, ...	2 0 0	James Hughes, ...	1 0 0
W. P. Grimshaw, ...	5 0 0	John Thompson, ...	2 0 0	William M'Ilwaine, ...	1 0 0
Robert Boyd, ...	5 0 0	John Louden, ...	2 0 0	William Speers, ...	1 0 0
Gordon Speer, ...	5 0 0	William Patterson, ...	2 0 0	Robert M'Calmont, ...	1 0 0
Robert Simpson, ...	5 0 0	Sarah Morrow, ...	2 0 0	David Ramsay, ...	1 0 0
George Greer, ...	5 0 0	John Giffen, ...	2 0 0	John Chisom, ...	1 0 0
William Chisom, ...	5 0 0	William Smyth, ...	2 0 0	George Mitchell, ...	1 0 0
Thomas Houston, ...	5 0 0	Isabella Boyd, ...	2 0 0	David Lewis, ...	1 0 0
William Rodgers, ...	2 0 0	William Tate, ...	2 0 0	John M'Cormick, ...	1 0 0
Hugh M'Kegherty, ...	2 0 0	Robert M'Ilwaine, ...	2 0 0	John Vint, ...	1 0 0
John Burney, ...	2 0 0	William Giffen, ...	2 0 0	David Harper, ...	1 0 0
George Smyth, ...	2 0 0	Thomas M'Kinney, ...	2 0 0	Thomas Higgins, ...	1 0 0

Reward poster, 1863, which lists the main farming families in the Carnmoney area.

over a field after which it was ploughed.

Besides all these crops, for both sale and domestic consumption, another 'product' of the land with which the McKinneys concerned themselves was turf. One June William McKinney records: 'Robert Robinson and I filled mud in the barrows at the King's Moss.' This was turf mud which was made into turf bricks. Elsewhere he refers to his father and ten men making turf at the King's Moss. The family continued to obtain turf from local bogs until the end of the century when all the bogs were used up. From the 1830s, however, they had been supplementing this source of fuel with coal from Whitehouse and Belfast.

During William's lifetime the family holding at Sentry Hill expanded and prospered greatly. This is clearly seen in the way in which the farm extended from 45 statute acres in 1832 to 92 acres by the last decade of the century. Besides the house at Sentry Hill they came to own the houses at Fairymount and Sunnyside. Clearly the hard work which they undertook

Diagram the Squares are in the same proportion as the Acres.

Irish Acre	Cuninghingham	English
7840 square yards.	6250 sq. yds.	4840 sq. y.
£1 · 0 · 0	£0 · 15 · 11½ +	£0 · 12 · 4½
1 · 5 · 1 +	1 · 0 · 0	0 · 15 · 5½ +
1 · 12 · 4½ +	1 · 5 · 10 -	1 · 0 · 0.

Designed by Thomas Blain, LL.D.
Head Master of the English Department in the Royal Belfast Academical Institution.

to improve the land and the energy which they expended to make the most out of their farm year by year, as their accounts and diaries demonstrate, were vital in this. Important as well was the care with which they managed their affairs – this the accounts also show. But these factors alone would not explain why they were successful. After all, the writer of the Ordnance Survey Memoir reckoned there were hardly any farmers in the district who could put their hands on £50 ready cash – and yet the McKinneys' acquisition of land was an extremely expensive business.

The £90 fine paid for the 1826 perpetuity lease on Sentry Hill was probably cheap because McKinney was a sitting tenant. But to purchase the one life and twenty-year lease for the Mallusk farm, Thomas George McKinney paid £146 and to buy the 1841 perpetuity lease he paid £975. The Fairymount lease cost £1123 and that for Sunnyside ran to £1300. In the case of these leases small half-yearly rents had still to be paid. How were they able to afford these costly acquisitions? Part of the answer to this question is that the McKinneys could obtain mortgages or loans from Belfast merchants and neighbours. In 1861, for example, William borrowed £600 from his friend Thomas Houston and the Belfast firm of Joseph Biggar at 5 per cent interest per annum. The considerable sums of interest and capital repayment which these purchases entailed may partly explain the hard work and constant improvements which the McKinneys carried out. It had been noted in the area in the 1830s that those with higher rents cultivated their land more, to meet the higher expenses. So, with such loan commitments, the McKinneys had to work hard and improve in order to meet their obligations.

Overleaf:
The East Antrim Hounds at Leigenfield, Mossley, 1895, shortly after their formation. Leigenfield was the largest farm in the area and was the home of the Chisolms. The formation of the hunt was a sign of the new self-confidence and prosperity of the farming community.

The most important factor, however, which encouraged the growth in prosperity and enabled the McKinneys to buy more land, was the rise in agricultural prices during this period. For example, by the early 1870s William McKinney obtained an average price of over 4s. per cwt for potatoes while his father in 1831 had received only around 2s. per cwt. Almost certainly William was producing more per acre than his father had because of land improvement and new techniques. New breeds of cows increased milk and butter yield. Some costs had gone up, in particular labour, but still his position by the 1870s was much better than his father's had been thirty-five years earlier. This prosperity did not continue at such a rate. Bad harvests in the years 1877 to 1880 and increased competition from abroad lowered profits. Temporary improvements occurred but by the 1890s prices were again falling. The first decade of the twentieth century saw something of an increase but not at the earlier level. Still, by 1914 the farm at Sentry Hill provided a good living for the family.

Robert Carlisle and his wife, both of whom worked at Sentry Hill, and Tom Couley, pig killer, 1900 (W.McK.).

Jenny Hill outside her family home at Ballycraigy, c.1895 (W.McK.). The Hills farmed about 30 acres and built this house in the 1880s to replace their earlier thatched cottage, seen in the background.

Sam and Susan Easton, *c.*1900 (W.McK.). After working as labourers at Fairymount, Sam and Susan married in 1870 and moved to Belfast where Sam obtained a job with a steamship company. They remained friendly with the McKinneys.

All these factors which affected the improvements and prosperity of the McKinneys were also, of course, important for the neighbourhood. Whereas in the 1830s the area had been described as being badly farmed, by the 1880s it was very different. Bassett's guide to Co. Antrim in 1888 described the district as a highly cultivated one. The amalgamation of farms, with the expansion of some farmers' buildings and the disappearance of others, resulted in a drop in the number of farming families. The McKinneys were clearly at the head of this development, occupying in the 1890s what had formerly been four separate holdings. Writing in 1884, McKinney observed the social changes that were occurring:

Joshua Wells, journeyman tailor, *c.*1900 (W.McK.). He was one of the many different types of craftsmen who travelled the countryside at this time. When he called at Sentry Hill to make clothes for the menfolk, he slept in one of the outhouses.

Farmers are decreasing in numbers, small farms that a few years ago sustained happy thriving families are now lying almost vacant. The farmer's family has disappeared and silence reigns in the homestead where once the voice of joy and gladness caused the welkin to ring. One man with the aid of machinery and modern farming implements can do more work than three or four men could have done 50 years ago and as there is no scope for using machinery on small farms and the old system at the present rate of wages won't pay, small farmers

are either going into business or emigrating. Those that remain are labouring what was formerly from two to six or eight farms.

By this stage the growth of industry was such that farming had long ceased to be the principal means of employment in the area. New mills were established at Whitehouse, Mallusk and Mossley.

So far, farming at Sentry Hill has been looked at very largely from the viewpoint of the McKinneys. But while they dominate the scene they are not the only actors in this story. There are also the labourers and the landlords. We have already noted (pp. 24–6) the references to the former in T.G. McKinney's wages ledger of 1835 and tried to guess something about the identity and character of these people as well as their conditions of work. For the second half of the century there is more information in William's diaries and account books.

On 12 May 1857, for example, McKinney notes:

The following is the wages that my father gives to the men:
G. Hume, £4.4.0 for 6 months
Thomas Robinson and David Thompson, 7s.0d. per week with perquisites.
Alexander Nesbit (a boy), £2 for 6 months
David Caldwell, 2s.0d. per day.

G. Hume and Alexander Nesbit almost certainly lived in at the farm but the others stayed out in cottages owned by the McKinneys. According to a rent book at Sentry Hill, in 1857 Caldwell rented a 'house, garden, 10 loads of earth and ground for manure' for £2.10.0; in previous years he had also rented some land: 'the west island field with grass of loanin from 12th May till 12th Nov 1855 – £3.0.0.' Caldwell continued to pay fifty shillings for his house until 1874 when it was raised to £3. The rent book mentions others such as Thomas Giffillan who rented at Mallusk 'a house, garden, 10 loads earth with ground for manure, grass of little field with as much shearing and cutting grass as sufficient to feed a cow' from 1

114

David Caldwell, labourer at Sentry Hill, *c.*1900 (W.McK.).

November 1851 to 1 November 1852 for £2. After Giffillan died, his widow moved to another McKinney house with the same conditions for a cheaper rent.

As the book indicates, these tenants could pay for their rents by work on the McKinney farm. Some worked full-time for them, but the remainder only at special times of the year; they would also have worked for other farmers. On occasions when a large amount of labour was required extra labourers were engaged. Entries in McKinney diaries for the 1850s and

1860s talk of twelve to fifteen women being employed by his father to pull flax or gather potatoes. The full-time labourers were normally hired for six months. Casual labourers were usually paid by the day but sometimes were paid for the work done. On 4 September 1852 McKinney writes: 'got done cutting the corn. John Lawther mowed all season and 6 or 8 others shore at 1 penny per stroke [stook] on the pea hill and West fauld'.

Besides the couple of male labourers who lived in at Sentry Hill in the 1850s there would also have been one or two resident female labourers, employed for either indoor or outdoor work. During this period McKinney makes many references to the people working on his father's farm. He records the death of David Thompson on 10 December 1857: 'David Thompson got a paralytic stroke in Mallusk meadow and died after he was taken home in the cart. He took a very hearty dinner and was singing as he went back to his work. He never spoke after he fell down in the meadow.' Three days later he writes: 'David Thompson was buried at Doagh. I gave 9s.0d. for a coffin for him.'

In October 1855 McKinney relates an incident concerning one of his next door neighbour's labourers:

> George McMillan's servant man came home from town drunk and commenced to abuse George and the girl. I went to the house and handcuffed him and then went with police who took him with them.

The servant served a summons on McKinney for assault and he had to appear at the Whitehouse Petty Sessions but the matter was dropped before it came up before the magistrates.

In 1861 William McKinney and his wife Elizabeth set up their new home at Fairymount. From his diaries it is clear that McKinney's first full-time worker was Sam Easton who seems to have lived with his family in the neighbourhood. His brother William provided part-time assistance. Then on 28 July 1862 McKinney records:

> Wrought in the house almost all day erecting a bed at the back of the shed for Susan Bailie who came this evening to live with us until Nov. at 50 shillings, & for 6 months.

There are many references over the next eight years to William McKinney, Sam Easton and Susan Bailie working together in the fields, occasionally with the help of others. On 8 October 1863 he writes: 'Sam, Susan and I crowned and roped the remainder of the stacks in the mid park before 1 o'c.' Susan helped not only with the churning but with most of the jobs in the fields. In December 1863 she obtained a form for a free passage for Melbourne but in the end burnt the papers. In January 1867 McKinney acquired for Susan and Sam account books with the savings bank. Eventually they were married in 1870 and moved to Belfast, but remained in close contact with the McKinneys.

On certain occasions, his father's casual workers helped out. In July 1864 eleven of Thomas's labourers pulled flax for William. The list of their

Unidentified maid at Sentry Hill, c.1905 (W.McK.).

117

Alic McIlwaine and child, c.1895.
Alic was first employed by the
McKinneys in 1886, and lived with
his family at Fairymount until his
death in the 1940s.

names shows many of them to have been wives and daughters of
McKinney cottagers while others are from farther afield. There are signs
that by the mid 1860s labourers were becoming more difficult to find,
probably because there were more attractive jobs elsewhere, such as in the
mills at Mossley and Hydepark. Writing to her two brothers-in-law, Hugh
and Joe, in 1866 Eliza McKinney remarked, 'We have two diggers at our
potatoes – it is hard to get workers at present'.

After the Eastons left, various other people were employed at Fairymount. Alex. Barkley was engaged in March 1873 but went off in August
to work for someone else; McKinney had a summons served on him to

HOUSES & LAND
FOR THE PEOPLE.

NOTICE.

EVERY
Workingman & Woman
(WITH FEW EXCEPTIONS)
IN THE PARISHES OF
CARNMONEY & TEMPLEPATRICK
IS ENTITLED TO AND
Can DEMAND a COTTAGE
as good as the new houses, "Cluainin" and "Cluainmel,"
built at BALLYVESEY,
WITH LAND
Not exceeding ONE ACRE at a CHEAP RENT.
If such Houses and Land are not given to the Workers
IT IS THEIR OWN FAULT.
The District Councillors for Carnmoney and Templepatrick **ARE
BOUND** TO SUPPLY THEM.
**The workers in every other Parish
have had such houses built for them.
Why not those of Carnmoney and Temple-
patrick, who are as good as any in
Ireland, and as well entitled to them?**
ERIE GO BRAT
Printed on Ballyclare Paper by P. Quinn, Church Street, Belfast.

This undated poster protesting against the lack of new labourers' dwellings in the Carnmoney area was found at Sentry Hill. 'Cluainin' and 'Cluainmel' were both built by F.J. Biggar.

bring him back. In 1874 he offered two men 13 shillings per week but they declined saying they would rather have 12 shillings and easy work – a reference perhaps to a factory job. McKinney's diaries during the 1870s and 1880s reflect a growing difficulty in getting workers to stay both at Sentry Hill and Fairymount. In May 1883 David Caldwell who had been receiving 12 shillings per week wanted 14 shillings but McKinney felt this was too much and Caldwell left along with another labourer who felt the same.

Later in 1883 McKinney went to a hiring fair at Carnmoney and obtained new helpers. David Caldwell eventually returned to work for the McKinneys as did his son, also called David. On 12 November 1886 McKinney notes the employment arrangements made by his son John.

John engaged Alic McIlwaine to live at Fairymount free of rent and to receive 12/– per week of wages. Old David Caldwell is also to receive 12/– per week and Johnny Porter who is 12 years old only £1.15/– for six months with board and lodging.

360.

Susan Moore also worked at Sentry Hill for £5 for six months. The younger Caldwell left in 1888 to become a postman – his new job paid 10s.10d. per week compared with the five shillings he received as a boy labourer.

By the last decades of the century, therefore, conditions for labourers had improved. Wages had risen considerably from the 1830s level, and housing also changed for the better. McKinney notes how in July 1884, Hugh Archbold, a neighbour, began work on new cottars' houses, no doubt encouraged by the recent government scheme to improve labourers' dwellings. From 1880 various workmen's compensation acts gave agricultural labourers certain rights in cases of injury: among the papers at Sentry Hill is an insurance policy taken out in 1901 by John McKinney in case of accidents on the farm. Yet by the 1880s people were less keen to become farm labourers than before, largely due to better pay and conditions elsewhere. Industrial housing was also often better than that provided for farm-workers. A report in *The Belfast Telegraph* (28 November 1978) on some 1880s millhouses at Whiteabbey revealed that

This labourer's cottage (known locally as the Sentry Box, as it was here that a sentry was supposed to have been positioned during the Williamite wars) on the brow of Sentry Hill was typical of the one-roomed cottages common in Ireland before the Famine. It survived here until the First World War and housed a large family. This photograph was taken *c*.1910 (W.McK.), by which time labourers' dwellings in general had improved.

120

these were amongst the first houses in the province to have had cavity wall construction. By this time there is little evidence of the large number of workers seen in the fields in the 1850s, thanks also to the new labour-saving machinery.

Finally there were the landlords. Unlike today, when most farmers own their farms, up to the end of the nineteenth century farmers in Ireland merely tenanted their holdings which were *owned* by landlords. Fortunately for the McKinneys, Sentry Hill was part of the vast Antrim estate owned by the Donegall family, who turned out to be one of the most dissolute and profligate of Irish aristocratic dynasties. Because of their enormous debts they were prepared in the early nineteenth century to sell off long-term rights on their property for immediate cash gain.

In 1826 then, Thomas George McKinney was able to buy a perpetuity lease for Sentry Hill. Such an arrangement was extremely beneficial for the

Samuel Anderson, here photographed by William McKinney, *c.*1895, held 29 acres at Ballycraigy, under a yearly tenancy from the Biggar family. William represented him and other farmers in the townland when their cases went before the new land courts in the 1880s.

Received this 3rd day of December 1877

from Thomas G. McKinney

the Sum of Nine pounds 11/6

for Half-a-Year's Rent due to **The Rev. ARTHUR PAKENHAM,**

at November 1877 (Rent)

out of a holding, No. 731 Mullusk

Cash, ... £	9	4	9
Poor Rate, ...		4	9
Income Tax, ...			
County Cess, ...			
Total, ... £	9	11	6

C. E. McClintock

N° 416

DONEGALL ESTATES.

Belfast, 12 Nov 1878.

Received from Mr Thomas Geo. McKinney

Two pounds 14/1 Sterling, being

half a years rent, due to the Most Honble The Marquis of Donegall

out of a holding in Ballyoisey

on the first day of November 1878. (Eight)

Rent	£	2. 14. 1		
Leets &c.		1. 0		
Poor Rate 10 .	2.3		2. 15. 1	
In. Tax 5° . —	1.1		. 3. 4	
Net	£	2. 11. 9		

for James Torrens

James Hannah

McKinney rent receipts.

122

tenant, because it allowed him almost complete security – he held the land in perpetuity so long as certain minor undertakings were fulfilled. Thomas McKinney had to pay the sum of £90 6s.5d. and undertake to pay a low annual rent of £5 7s.6d., and, rather peculiarly, a small fixed payment on the death of certain named members of the Donegall family. McKinney probably obtained the lease cheaply because he was a sitting tenant and the Donegalls needed the money urgently. When a neighbouring farm with a similar acreage came on the open market fourteen years later, McKinney was prepared to pay £975 for it.

McKinney had been lucky with Sentry Hill. While he was able to buy his own lease directly from the landlord, large acreages of the Donegall lands in the area were usually sold to middlemen and then rented to farmers either on short-term leases or yearly tenancies. By the 1830s about half of Ballyvesey was tenanted by farmers on perpetuity leases from Donegall but the rest was held by the Crawford family of Belfast who let the land out to farmers.

The McKinneys' other farm at Mallusk was held under a medium-term lease. The Pakenham family owned most of the adjacent parish of Templepatrick which included Mallusk. The lease which Thomas McKinney bought from Mathew Biggar, in 1826, for the sum of £146 was for twenty years or the lifetime of C.R. Dobbs of Castle Dobbs (near Carrickfergus), whichever term was the longer. This type of arrangement may seem rather strange today but was perfectly normal in the nineteenth century. The term could be based on several persons' lives and problems sometimes arose because the persons named might move away and no-one would know whether or not they had died. It meant of course that keen attention was paid to the health of those particular individuals! Fortunately for the McKinneys, Dobbs lived until 1886.

There was therefore considerable variety in the way the land was let at Sentry Hill and in the neighbourhood. The perpetuity lease was the most favourable arrangement for the farmer, while the yearly tenancy (the type generally found in the rest of Ireland in the nineteenth century) was the least favourable. In theory the yearly tenant had few rights, although in many parts of Ulster, and elsewhere, in practice he was allowed to remain undisturbed on his holding as long as the rent was paid. He could sell his right of occupancy, taking into account any improvements he had made. The Ulster Custom, as these unwritten rights of the tenant were known, seems to have been observed fully in this area and the tenants enjoyed all the advantages of the rise in prices for agricultural goods.

Although the landlord occupied an important place in rural society, the Donegall family made little impact in East Antrim, no doubt because they had sold off so much of their land and also because they did not reside in the area. The Pakenham family, who did live locally, had much more influence. During the 1850s, both William McKinney and his father attended dinners in honour of their Mallusk landlord, Rev. A.H. Pakenham. In 1859, for example, the tenants on the Pakenham estate

entertained their landlord and his brother, Lt Col. T.H. Pakenham, MP for the county, at 'a public complimentary dinner in Crumlin, as a mark of the respect and esteem with which they are universally regarded'. As well as speeches, an address was presented to the Pakenhams, which paid tribute to their good qualities and incidentally spelt out what the tenants expected and received from their landlords. References were made to the Pakenhams recognising 'the just rights of the tenantry' and 'never having taken advantage of the improvements effected by them'. Twice a year, in May and November, one of the McKinneys delivered the rent to the Pakenham agent at Langford Lodge, on the shores of Lough Neagh.

This picture of landlord-tenant relations in the area is a fairly amicable one, but there were certain underlying sources of tension. The great variety in tenurial arrangements, which might benefit some tenants but not others, may itself have been a cause of irritation. More importantly, the positions of yearly and short-term tenants were not secure. While local landlords like the Pakenhams recognised the Ulster Custom, the mere fact that tenants' rights were not legal but only customary ones and could be (and sometimes were) overlooked must have caused a sense of uncertainty and insecurity.

In a book of newspaper cuttings collected by William McKinney is an

Sunnyside garden, c.1900 (W.McK.). John and Catherine McKinney lived there from 1890 to her death in 1896 when it was sold to the McMeekin family. Mrs McMeekin is in the background. It is interesting to compare this house, which has been rebuilt and extended, with that of the McCrums', *opposite*, which has not. Both farms were in the same townland, with roughly similar acreages, but Sunnyside had been held on a perpetuity lease since the early nineteenth century, while the McCrums' was held on short-term leases or yearly tenancies. The degree of security felt by tenants undoubtedly affected the improvements they made to their homes.

James McCrum and family, Ballyvesey, c.1895 (W.McK.). James McCrum rented his 40 acres from the Crawford family. McCrum's people had originally come from Scotland in the early eighteenth century. James McCrum was an elder of the local Presbyterian church and superintendent of Ballycraigy sabbath school.

account of a court case in 1859 involving a tenant on the nearby Dobbs estate who was put off his farm without compensation. A new land agent had arrived on the estate without knowledge or sympathy for any unwritten land right. He decided to remove some tenants from their holdings and refused them leave to sell their occupancy rights to the next tenants. An appeal against the eviction was dismissed at the Belfast Quarter Sessions on the grounds that the tenants had no legal right to their claim.

When, in 1864, the Henry Joy estate which included part of neighbouring Ballyhenry was sold, the tenants sent a representative (Dr John Dundee, Isaac Dundee's father) to bid for them at the sale in Dublin. Dundee was outbid by Joseph Biggar (a Belfast pork merchant and father of the home rule MP Joe Biggar) and later claimed that Biggar had offered to drop out of the bidding in return for £100 which he had of course refused to pay. Once he took over, Biggar increased the rents on the Ballyhenry farms by nearly 50 per cent. This may have been a fair increase, in keeping with the general rise in prices since the land was first let, but it was deeply resented by the tenants, who obviously feared that it could happen again.

If and when rises occurred, the final say lay with the landlord. The

The three Guthrie brothers in front of their cottage at the King's Moss. Note the paved area, known as the causeway or 'cassie', in front of the house.

tenant could therefore be faced with a quite arbitrary decision for a new rent which might be difficult to pay. When a number of 21-year leases in the neighbourhood expired in 1863, the owner, the Rev. Archibald Crawford, fixed new rents on the advice of his valuator. These were generally 50 per cent above the old rents, but the Campbell family had theirs increased considerably more, and this drove them, eighteen years later, to one of the new land courts which had been set up to settle fair rents. Isabella Simms Campbell gave evidence of her position:

The farm which I hold contains 5a[cres] 3r[ods] 35p[erches] statute measure, or the 'wee acre' as it is called. One of my boys is a smith and the other is a yarn bundler. Neither of the two drinks, for it took all the money they could get to keep them. At the present rate what grew on the farm would not give us potatoes

William Macartney with his two daughters at Killyreel, 1899 (W.McK.). He was 101 years old when this photograph was taken. After the Land Act of 1881 the rent for the 7 acres he held under the Pakenham family was reduced from £5 to £3.17s.0d. A newspaper report about him on his 101st birthday described him as being very deaf, but 'sometimes in a very excited state when called on for rent or taxes'.

and buttermilk and we cannot live on that always. Before the year 1866 the rent was £5.15. but now it was £9.4.0d.

The Rogers family in front of their home at Ballyduff. Eleven acres were attached to their farm.

Despite the hardship occasioned by this increased rent, she agreed, reluctantly, to pay it:

When my husband died the housing was in very bad repair but since the children grew up it has been much improved. The landlord never spent any money on the farm. I was noticed regarding a rise of rent by the agent, I believe, Mr McAuliffe. I agreed to pay the rise and was glad to do so because it was still a home for me. I paid the increase rather than flit, for country people don't like flitting. They always like to stay in the old den. After I paid the rent, I told them [the family] when I got home that we would get living another year yet.

This was an extreme case and such incidents did not often happen, but the

Thomas McClenaghan and family, Ballycraigy, *c*.1900 (W.McK.). Their farm extended to 24 acres.

possibility was always there, and it was the uncertainty caused by such actions that created later unrest.

The Liberal tenant-right movement which began in 1869 had the full support of both William McKinney and his father. This was probably not just a result of concern about tenurial rights but also served as a protest against the dominant role of the landlords in rural society. There may also have been a small element of religious conflict here: the landlords were nearly all Church of Ireland while most of the Protestant tenant farmers who supported land reform were Presbyterians.

Bad harvests in the late 1870s and growing competition from abroad led to severe unrest throughout Ireland in the years 1879–81. The 1881 Land Act legalised fixity of tenure, a system of fair rents and compensation to tenants for improvements. Land courts were set up to deal with difficulties over these matters. During the next four years William McKinney attended the land courts on a number of sessions, sometimes as a witness and sometimes representing groups of tenants in his neighbourhood.

In 1888, however, he appeared on his own behalf. Two years previously the person named as the 'life' in his Mallusk farm lease had died and within twelve months Pakenham's agent proposed to raise the rent from its 1809 level of £9.11s.6d. to £10.14s.2d. McKinney referred the new rent to the land court, arguing, first, that the land had been improved from mere swamp land to good farming land thanks only to his father's efforts, and, second, that by 1888 prices had fallen while labour had become much more expensive. Strictly speaking, McKinney was correct in all these points but at the same time it was not unreasonable for Pakenham to have sought a rise at this much later stage. Because of the drop in prices, the rise in rent may not have been entirely unwarranted at this stage but because of the considerable rise in prices in previous years the McKinneys had done

Backyard at Sentry Hill, *c.*1895 (W.McK.). The boy is seated on the steps which were used for mounting a horse. To the left can be seen the potato shed.

1888.

Templepatrick Petty Sessions Court.

IN MEMORIAM.

CARSON *VERSUS* PERRY.

WHO fraudulently altered a certain valuation,
    For the mere purpose of extortation,
To ensure my being kicked out of occupation?
              Captain Perry!

Who, by trickery, fraud, and sheer deception,
And by fraudulent representation,
Altered Watters's valuation?
              Captain Perry!

When I asked for, who refused me arbitration,
So as to rob me of honest compensation,
Who forced me from my home and habitation?
              Captain Perry!

Who robbed me of character, credit and reputation,
Who almost drove me to starvation,
And refused to hold any further negotiation?
              Captain Perry!

Who is the hero of evictions,
Of Boycotting, cheating, and confiscations,
Of coercion and misrepresentations,
              Captain Perry!

By whose hands suffered I such excruciation,
Who strove to drive me to desolation,
The greatest scoundrel in all creation—
              Captain Perry!

Captain Perry, attacked in this anonymous broadsheet, was probably a local land agent.

very well out of the arrangement. The court allowed a compromise rent of £10.10s.0d.

By the mid 1880s the antagonism between landlord and tenant had abated, partly because the Land Act ironed out problems in their relationship and partly because the home rule threat made them come together. As evidence we can notice that in 1888 one of the Pakenhams was invited to lay the foundation stone for the new Presbyterian church at Lyle Hill. The Pakenhams and other local gentry also acted as patrons for the grand fête held at Carnmoney in 1893 in aid of the proposed Presbyterian Hall. But the political turmoil of the 1870s and 1880s had altered their position in a way that could not be forgotten. The County Council Act of 1898 abolished the grand juries which had previously given the landlords control of local government and established elected county councils. Land purchase had already begun in the 1880s but the Wyndham Act of 1903 was to give widespread facilities for land purchase. In 1904 the McKinneys bought out their Mallusk land – as did most of the other Pakenham tenants, leaving their former landlord with only his demesne. So by the First World War, the McKinneys were in complete control of all their land at Sentry Hill and in the vicinity.

5
Adventures Abroad

Among William McKinney's papers at Sentry Hill are some notes from a paper which he delivered to Carnmoney Mutual Improvement Society on the subject of emigration. He dwelt on the sad loss to families of sons and daughters who emigrated to foreign lands and maintained that they should stay at home to develop Ireland's own resources. He did believe, however, that there were other members of the community who might more easily be spared, notably the gentry and members of the clergy, whether Catholic or Church of Ireland. (Presbyterian ministers were not, of course, included in this!) Certainly the McKinney circle experienced this loss through emigration in the second half of the nineteenth century: four of William's brothers and sisters went overseas as did four of his own children. At the same time, however, the resources and opportunities of these new nations were much greater than could be found at home and the emigrants achieved a lot more than would have been possible in Ireland.

The first member of William McKinney's circle to go abroad was Joseph McGaw of Sunnyside in 1856. (It was his sister Eliza whom William was to marry five years later, and the connection was reinforced when Joseph's brother, William John, married Sarah McKinney.) Joseph's correspondence home was kept, and later copied down by William McKinney. It shows the hardships which emigration often involved and also the chances it provided for advancement. McGaw sailed from Liverpool in October 1856. His arrival in Australia some six weeks later was described in a letter dated 9 December:

Landed at Melbourne today at ½ past 2 o'c. P.M. There were only 3 deaths on board. Joseph Alexander met us at the wharf. I met with a very kind reception from him and his wife. Saw a gang of convicts at work on the banks of the Yarra cutting thistles. Two policemen armed with rifles were with them.

He lodged with the Alexander family and began work on his second day at a general store run by a Belfast man: 'I am working everyday with pork and hams from Richardson, Waring & Coey of Belfast'. A few months later he took a job as an assistant to a surveyor.

Letters from surveyors' camps in the bush sketch harsh working conditions. They also show his amazement at this strange new environment. On 28 March 1857 he wrote from a camp at Tower Hill: 'I have made a rug for my bed of possum skins. The sandflies and mosquitoes are very troublesome. The swamp water that we use is green like a duck pond.'

Journey to Australia, 1865 style.

"BLACK BALL" & "EAGLE"

LINE OF BRITISH AND AUSTRALIAN EX-ROYAL MAIL PACKETS.

This Line of Celebrated Steam and Clipper Ships is the only one that has had the distinguished honour of a visit from HER MAJESTY THE QUEEN.

Great Victoria, s.s.
Great Britain, s.s.
Golden Land
Golden City
City of Melbourne
Light of the Age
Light Brigade
Queen of the Colonies
Queen of the South
Champion of the Seas
Blanche Moore
Elizabeth Ann Bright

Donald Mackay
Commodore Perry
Royal Dane
Ocean Chief
Young England
British Trident
Sunda
Lightning
Marco Polo
Flying Cloud
Fiery Star
Maryborough

The above Fleet is composed of the Largest, Finest, and Fastest Ships in the World.

NOW LOADING IN COBURG DOCK.

LIVERPOOL TO MELBOURNE,

FORWARDING PASSENGERS TO GEELONG, SYDNEY, ADELAIDE, HOBART TOWN, AND LAUNCESTON.

PACKET FOR THE 5TH APRIL, 1865,

THE CELEBRATED CLIPPER SHIP

SAMARANG

1,175 Tons Register, 3,000 Tons Burthen; Captain Richardson.

Rates of Passage.

	MELBOURNE.	SYDNEY.	HOBART TOWN AND LAUNCESTON.	ADELAIDE.
SALOON CABIN,	£45 0 0	£50 0 0	£50 0 0	£50 0 0
INTERMEDIATE,	17 0 0	20 0 0	20 0 0	20 0 0
STEERAGE,	15 0 0	18 0 0	18 0 0	19 0 0

All Passengers in the INTERMEDIATE and STEERAGE will have to provide themselves with Bed and Bedding, a Knife and Fork each, 1 Table Spoon, 1 Tea Spoon, 1 Tin Plate, Drinking Can, 1 Tin Quart and Pint Pot, 1 Slop Pail, and a Keg or Can for holding Water. The whole can be had for 21s. at Mr. GEORGE PERCIVAL'S Stores, 23, Bath-street, Liverpool.

CHILDREN UNDER TWELVE YEARS, HALF-FARE. INFANTS UNDER TWELVE MONTHS, FREE.

EACH SHIP CARRIES AN EXPERIENCED SURGEON.

DIETARY SCALE FOR EACH ADULT PASSENGER PER WEEK.

ARTICLES.	Intermediate.	Steerage.	ARTICLES.	Intermediate.	Steerage.	ARTICLES.	Intermediate.	Steerage.
Biscuits	$3\frac{1}{2}$ lbs.	$3\frac{1}{2}$ lbs.	Oatmeal	1 lb.	1 lb.	Butter	6 oz.	4 oz.
Beef	$1\frac{1}{4}$,,	$1\frac{1}{4}$,,	Raisins	8 oz.	8 oz.	Pickles and Vinegar	$1\frac{1}{2}$ gill.	1 gill.
Pork	1 ,,	1 ,,	Suet	6 ,,	6 ,,	Salt	2 oz.	2 oz.
Preserved Meats	1 ,,	1 ,,	Tea	2 ,,	2 ,,	Mustard	$\frac{1}{2}$,,	$\frac{1}{2}$,,
Flour	$2\frac{1}{2}$,,	2 ,,	Coffee	2 ,,	....	Pepper	$\frac{1}{2}$,,	$\frac{1}{4}$,,
Peas	1 ,,	$1\frac{1}{2}$,,	Sugar	1 lb.	1 lb.	Treacle	$\frac{1}{4}$ lb.	....
Rice	$\frac{1}{2}$,,	$\frac{1}{2}$,,	Loaf Sugar	....	....	Water	21 qts.	21 qts.
Potatoes, Preserved	$\frac{1}{2}$,,	$\frac{1}{2}$,,	Cheese	....	....	Lime Juice	6 oz.	6 oz.

Passengers are found according to the above Dietary Scale, and not by that in the Contract Ticket.

At the option of the Master of the Ship the following Substitutions may be made in the Dietary Scale:—1 lb. Preserved Meat for 1 lb. Salt Pork or Beef; 1 lb. of Flour or of Bread, or $\frac{1}{2}$ lb. of Beef or of Pork, for $1\frac{1}{4}$ lb. of Oatmeal, or 1 lb. of Rice, or 1 lb. of Peas; 1 lb. of Rice for $1\frac{1}{4}$ lb. of Oatmeal, or *vice versa*; $\frac{1}{4}$ lb. of Preserved Potatoes for 1 lb. of Potatoes; 10 oz. of Currants for 8 oz. of Raisins; $3\frac{1}{2}$ oz. of Coffee, roasted and ground, for 2 oz. of Tea; $\frac{3}{4}$ lb. of Treacle for $\frac{1}{2}$ lb of Sugar; 1 gill of Mixed Pickles for 1 gill of Vinegar.

When Fresh Beef is issued, 1 lb. to each adult per day will be allowed; there will be no Flour, Rice, Raisins, Peas, Suet, or Vinegar, during the issue of Fresh Meat.

Children between one and twelve, one half the above allowance. Infants under one year to have one quart of Water Daily, but no rations.

Wines, Spirits, and Malt Liquors, under limitation by the Captain and the Passengers' Act, are supplied on board at moderate prices.

LUGGAGE.

Saloon Passengers are allowed 40 cubic feet; Second Cabin, 30 feet; the other classes of Passengers, 20 feet each; which must be made up in packages not exceeding 2 ft. 6 in. by 1 foot 6 in. wide, and 16 inches deep; freight on any excess will be charged 2s. 6d. per foot, and no package of greater bulk will be taken in the berths. Packages for the hold are not limited to any particular dimensions, but passengers are recommended to have them made as small as possible, as such will be found much more convenient on arrival at the Colony than large packages, which it may cost considerable expense to have removed. Passengers, should, for their own protection, have their names PAINTED legibly upon all Packages of Luggage, also in plain large characters the name of the Port they engage for.

The Ship will not be responsible for loss or damage of Luggage. Merchandise cannot be carried as Luggage.

Passengers having their Luggage in excess of their allowance will please give notice to the Agents to that effect, in order that room may be reserved. All packages of Baggage to be marked with the name of the Passenger, and also with the words "*Wanted on the Voyage,*" or "*Not Wanted on the Voyage.*"

No Passengers will be allowed to put their Luggage on board until the remainder of their Passage and extra Luggage charge has been settled. Passengers are expected to look after the shipment of their own Luggage, and to see it put on board the Vessel, and also to take charge of it when on board.

CASH ORDERS ON MELBOURNE FOR £1 AND UPWARDS ISSUED FREE OF CHARGE.

Agents in Melbourne—**BRIGHT, BROTHERS & CO., 36, Flinders' Lane West.**

For further particulars apply to JAMES BAINES & CO., Tower Buildings, Water Street; GIBBS, BRIGHT & CO., 1, North John Street, Liverpool; T. M. MACKAY & CO., 1, Leadenhall Street, London, E.C. or to

Samuel Gowan and Co., 4, Corporation-street, Belfast.

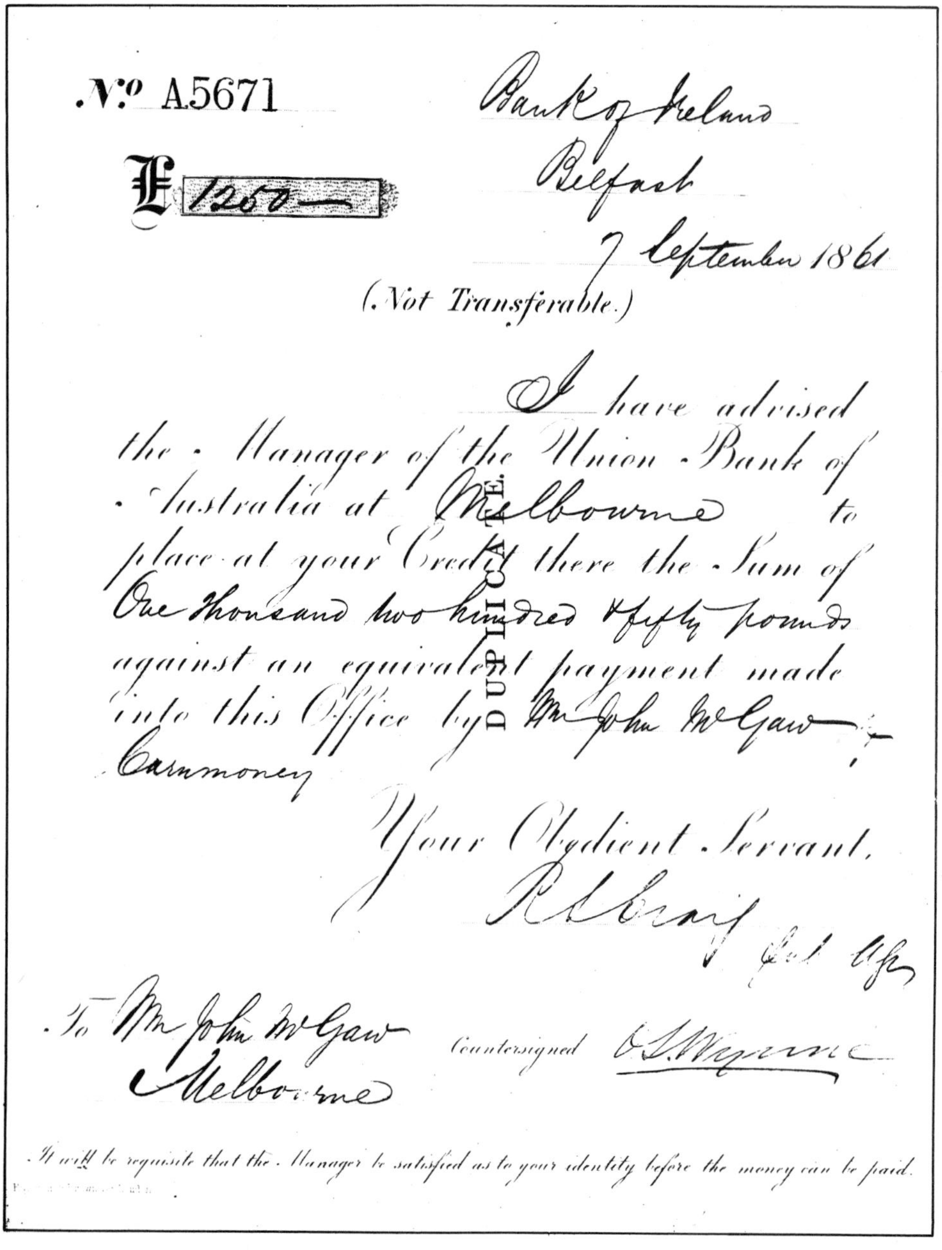

N.º A5671

£ 1250 —

Bank of Ireland
Belfast
7 September 1861

(Not Transferable.)

I have advised the Manager of the Union Bank of Australia at Melbourne to place at your Credit there the Sum of One thousand two hundred & fifty pounds against an equivalent payment made into this Office by Mr John McGaw, Carnmoney

Your Obedient Servant,

DUPLICATE

To Mr John McGaw
Melbourne

Countersigned

It will be requisite that the Manager be satisfied as to your identity before the money can be paid.

That Christmas Day he saw:

. . . cherry trees 20 ft high, 8 ft of stem. The stones are on the outside of the cherries. The hot north wind seemed to be coming off a red hot furnace. It howled in the branches of the trees tearing off the leaves and rotten boughs, making it dangerous to walk about. Mr Moore shot an emu. It weighed over 1 cwt.

Money order sent to Joe McGaw after sale of Fairymount to William McKinney, 1861.

During this time he frequently sent home examples of unusual bird and animal skins. Finally in March 1858 he gave up his job and accepted the post of overseer at the sheep station run by a David Wilson, another Co. Antrim man, for £70 per annum. He rode for five days to reach his new place of work: 'I camped out every night as I travelled by compass without regard to roads and never had an opportunity of stopping at a station.'

For the next seven years Joseph McGaw was to remain at Wilson's sheep farm on the Avon Plains. In one of his first letters home he describes the station there:

> David and I live together. We have a good house, walls papered, floor carpeted and everything tidy. We have plenty of books. We are 47 miles from the nearest meeting house . . . Most of the men are convicts. They receive 17/- per week with rations. The weekly rations are 10 lbs flour, 1 lbs sugar, ¼ lb tea and as much mutton as they can eat.

Life on the outstations tended to be less comfortable. On 25 June he writes:

> I am very lonely here now, no letters, no newspapers and working hard. I am living in a tent alone about twelve miles from the home station. I have 7 men out with me. My tent is about 9 by 7 in which I have a bag of flour, sugar, tea and a spare bed for strangers.

By 1859, however, he was in sole charge of the station and he clearly found the work rewarding and challenging. The following May, encouraged by reports of high prices for land in Carnmoney and good investment opportunities in Australia (8 per cent return on money invested as opposed to under 4 per cent in Belfast) he wrote home: 'I would like to sell my share of the farm . . . I would never think of buying a small farm again.' In September 1861, with the sale completed to W. F. McKinney, £1,250 was dispatched to him from Belfast. A month later he commented: 'I am glad to learn that I have no property in Ireland.' By February 1862 he was in charge of another Wilson farm, the Yanko station, in New South Wales. On its 240,000 acres there were 100 men employed to look after 27,000 sheep.

By the end of that year McGaw was earning £400 per annum: 'I have now more money than ever I expected to have.' His brother, William John, and some men from the Carnmoney area came out to work for him. Letters home tell of the heavy work and the enormous flocks of sheep. On 19 May 1864 he wrote:

> The lambing season has now fairly set in. I have 34,000 lambing in paddocks. Six men can attend to them. These would have required 50 men if lambed by hand. The lambing will be over in three weeks. Then marking the lambs commences; after that is got over preparation for shearing begins.

Later that year he was given a share in the farm, a clear sign of how his management was valued. But this did not work out to his satisfaction and in December 1865 he left Wilson to enter into a partnership with some others, including a John Cochrane from Coleraine, to purchase the

Burrabogie station for £110,000. Joseph McGaw was responsible for running the station, and as its 350,000 acres were not well developed, the early days involved a lot of hard work. On 1 July 1866 he described building a new home station: 'we live in tents and sleep on bags of flour, sugar etc.' At this point he had been ten years in Australia and sometimes felt that he might have returned home, 'but it would take years to work myself into the same position again'. (By 1867 he was responsible for 118,000 sheep and his share in the farm was worth about £15,000.)

Work on the sheep station involved not only taking care of the lambing and shearing but also making fences – a somewhat more arduous job than in Ballyvesey! On 18 May 1867 he wrote to his sister Eliza:

Wm Barklimore has been ploughing round fences with 10 or 12 bullocks for two or three months and has still two months work in that line to do yet. Andrew Campbell and party shovel the furrows from both sides under the wire of the fence which makes a bank about 14 inches high. I have got 100 miles of fencing made since last shearing at a cost of about £55 per mile, by which we save the cost of at least 45 shepherds at a cost of £50 each and rations per man about £26 amounting to say £3000 per annum.

In his letters he mentions the various problems which sometimes arose: a plague of grasshoppers on one occasion and a multitude of black caterpillars on another. Unlike Ireland, rain was eagerly looked for. Bush-rangers were a frequent threat. In 1865 Joseph was warned to expect a 'visit' from one notorious bush-ranger called Morgan, and spent some time practising shooting at a target with a revolver. The gun went off in his hand but fortunately he was not hurt, and as it happened, Morgan was killed by someone else before he ever reached Burrabogie.

On one occasion in 1867 he records riding eighty miles with 'no refreshment except a glass of wine at the end of 60 miles and would have taken nothing only I was pressed by a friend'. This was the man whom his brother had described a few years earlier: 'He does not shave and does not smoke, and is an advocate of temperance'.

This hardy, outdoor life was a rewarding and interesting one but it did have its drawbacks. In August 1857, while in the surveyors' camp at Spring Creek, he had written home: 'I have not seen a female for six weeks'. Eight years later, he wrote asking his sister to 'bespeak a sweetheart for me to be ready in two or three years, but not too young, as I am now getting grey haired'. But by 10 July 1866 he had had a change of heart:

The clergyman's wife was here, and is a very nice person, but her children almost drove me crazy. You need not trouble trying to get a wife to come to me as I am clean rued, since I had to put up these children for a night.

Three years later, however, he met and married a Miss Fanny MacNeill, one of eleven sisters from Ballycastle, Co. Antrim.

In 1872 he bought a half share in another station, Kooba, in the Lachlan district of New South Wales. Although he had relatively little money when

Joseph McGaw on a brief visit to Sunnyside, the former McGaw home, 1891 (W.McK.). *Left to right, back row:* Janet McKinney, John McKinney, Ninie McGaw, Catherine McKinney; *middle row:* Fanny and Joseph McGaw, Mrs Archbold; *front row:* Meg McKinney, Madeleine McGaw.

This newspaper extract describes the Burrabogie Station in the 1870s after it has been developed. By this stage there were only 227,824 acres attached to it.

Burrabogie Station—Murrumbidgee River, N.S.W.

Burrabogie is said to be a compound aboriginal word, and is translated as "Burra" quick, and "bogie" swim. The station is made up of six distinct leaseholds, or runs, embracing an area of 500 square miles. The station has a direct river frontage of 22 miles, or with bends 40 miles, and extends for 25 miles back. The whole of the vast area is fenced in and subdivided into 49 paddocks, ranging from 40 acres to 10,000 acres in extent. Upwards of 350 miles of sheep-proof fencing have been erected at a cost ranging from £50 to £80 per mile.

On Burrabogie there are 140,000 sheep. The superior character of those may be judged by a glance at the side-board in Burrabogie House, which is well filled with cups and champion prizes obtained at the Riverina Pastoral Shows. To improve the flocks still further, several stud rams have been imported at long prices—as high as £210 having been paid for one animal. In addition to the sheep there is also kept a small herd of 200 head of choice cattle. A portion of the station is set apart for a stud farm, where the pure merino sheep and short-horn cattle are kept. An addition has lately been made to the cattle stock by the purchase of a bull from the Nepean Towers herd at a cost of 400 guineas. A boiling-down establishment is also erected, capable of melting 2000 to 3000 sheep per week. This has not been used for several years, but it is said is likely to start shortly, as in the opinion of many stockholders, fat stock is rapidly reaching boiling-down price in that part of the colony.

Two steam-engines are constantly employed on the station, sawing timber for the numerous improvements going on, and in raising water for the use of the stock.

The station is worked on an excellent plan. Beside the head station there are eight out-stations, and twenty accommodation huts for the people employed.

The station requires about fifty constant hands, independent of the men employed by the contractors in fencing, dam-making, &c. At shearing time about 200 men are employed.

Burrabogie House is one of the finest in Riverina. Shearers, shepherds, and others define it as "the swell place" of that part of Riverina. The residence has spacious and lofty apartments, the whole well designed and well arranged. The garden and shrubbery are excellently kept. The grounds are arranged with considerable taste, and the trellis-worked avenue covered with vines proves a great boon in the heat of summer. The kitchens, stores, blacksmiths' and carpenters' shops, overseers and men's quarters, stables, coach houses, and other outbuildings at the head station, cover an area of two acres, and are of a first-rate character, being both substantial and ornamental. The present spirited proprietors have expended upwards of £40,000 during the past six years in improvements.

he started his first partnership he was able to build up capital because, in return for management of these estates, he received not only a salary but also a percentage of the profits; with this money and borrowed cash he built up his share of the partnerships in which he was involved. There was a lot of work and money involved in the sheep farming. On 2 October 1871 he recorded that they had shorn 115,000 sheep in twenty-nine days. In January 1872 he estimated that in the previous year he had received a return of 25 per cent on money invested and in October 1872 he could report back home that they had 1400 bales of wool worth £44,000. When the partnership ended in July 1878 Joseph bought the whole station – 104,000 acres of freehold land, 79,816 sheep, 700 cattle, 100 horses and considerable station plant, stores and furniture – for £235,000. He still managed the Burrabogie station and had a third share in its 227,824 acres and around 140,000 sheep. So by 1878 Joseph McGaw controlled nearly a third of a million acres, nearly half the acreage of Co. Antrim.

In 1882 Burrabogie was sold for £440,000. In spite of all this wealth, however, McGaw was still careful with money. On 21 October 1882 he wrote to William McKinney urging him to buy the Sunnyside farm at Ballyvesey which had just come on the market: 'If you can *buy* it at *what you consider a fair value* I will send the money home as soon as possible.' He obviously did not consider the asking price a fair one, for the farm was lost to another bidder. It was not until the 1890s that the McKinneys gained possession of Sunnyside. In late 1883 he returned to the British Isles and after a brief visit to Carnmoney set up home in England where he died in 1894.

The next member of the McKinney family to go abroad was William himself. Why he went is unclear. He may have felt that it would be some considerable time before he would gain control of the family farm. In early 1860 he gave up his positions in the church and temperance society and obtained character references not only from the Presbyterian minister but also from the Church of Ireland rector and the Congregational minister – obviously playing very safe! Then, as he noted in his diary on 6 March 1860, 'gave £6.6.0 for a berth in the *Kangeroo* from Queenstown to New York. Left Belfast in the 4 o'clock train and arrived in Dublin at 10'. He travelled on to Queenstown (Cobh) the next day and embarked. After seventeen days at sea the ship arrived in New York but was briefly held up before they could leave: on 6 April 1867, he recorded:

The quarantine doctor came on board and caused the ship to be stopped on account of a child on board having smallpox. Two doctors came on board after noon and vaccinated the crew and passengers. Some of the wild Irish kept a great noise about it. There were two Revenue Officers came on board and danced with the Corkonians.

He arrived in Ottawa on 12 April and drove to the home of a Presbyterian minister, a Mr Wardrope, who was able to fix him up immediately in lodgings and find him a job with a T. McKay of New

Edinburgh. The next day he began ploughing on McKay's farm, a job he was well used to, although not perhaps in such cold conditions: according to his diaries, 14 April was 'a very cold morning. There were icicles at the horse's nose'. He worked for McKay for the next five months during which time he became very friendly with Rev. Mr Wardrope and other members of the congregation. He taught in the Sabbath school and attended singing classes and prayer meetings. In his spare time he visited Ottawa and saw some of the sights.

In August 1860 McKinney commenced work in a saw mill and moved to new accommodation although still in the same area. He continued to correspond with home and sometimes purchased books. On 8 September 1860 he 'gave $1.25 for Gibson's *Year of Grace*, 90 cents for a map of Ottawa, 90 cents for a French bible, 50 cents for views of New York and Niagara and 35 cents for a French book.' Arrival of the snow in November brought pleasures and problems. Later that month he wrote: 'I got my first ride on a sleigh. There are great numbers skating.' The temperature dropped to 40 degrees below freezing. It was a sign of improvement when he could record: 'The pump was not frozen this morning [27 March 1861] for the first time.'

In February 1861 his father wrote asking him to come home. He remained in Canada for a while, perhaps unable to make up his mind what

Ambrotype portrait of William McKinney, taken in Canada.

MR WILLIAM F. MCKINNEY.

Ottawa City, Canada
April 27th 1861.

Dear Sir,

We the undersigned scholars in Knox Church Sabbath School attending your class, – hearing that you are about to take your departure from among us for your native land, beg leave to present you with the accompanying testimonial of our respect for you, and of our appreciation of your efforts to advance our knowledge of the sacred scriptures, and of the great saving truths which they contain.

The time that has elapsed since you began to instruct us (now about one year) seems very short. We regret that the connection between us of Teacher and Scholars, is so soon to expire in consequence of your determination to recross the Atlantic, but as you go, you will have our earnest prayers on your behalf addressed to our Divine Teacher, whom seas and winds obey, and to the God and Father of our Lord Jesus Christ, for your safety and protection while on the bosom of the mighty waters.

You will also carry with you our best wishes for your happiness and success in your future sphere of duty.

Hoping that your voyage across the ocean may be so prosperous, that we may soon hear from you, and that at the termination of the voyage of life (should it not be our lot to meet on earth again) we may meet among the abodes of the blessed.

We for the present bid you an affectionate farewell.

Thomas J. Ash	Charles Lazure	Columbus Ogleson
John Angus	Louis Lazure	Frederick Clemenhagen
William M'Intosh	John K. Stewart	Albert Clemenhagen
Frank Proderick	Robert Stewart	Robert Young
William Stewart	James Peterkin	James Young

A farewell address to William McKinney from his Canadian class.

Photograph taken at Fairymount in 1870 when William John and Sarah McGaw visited the McKinney family before departing for Australia (H.).

to do, and also restricted in movement by the freezing of the rivers. Finally, in May 1861, he took the *S.S. Bohemian* for Ireland. He recorded the scene at the beginning of his journey:

> Met about 200 ships bound for Quebec and Montreal. There were sometimes 40 in view at one time. Some of the officers on board said that they never saw so many large ships sailing in the same direction in so short a time.

The journey went smoothly although on 20 May, 'A complaint about the bill of fare was sent to the captain'. Two days later, Ireland was sighted: 'Came in sight of land at 8 o'clock during a fog. After we turned and steered north. The Londonderry boat met us at half past 4.' McKinney was to remain in Ireland for the rest of his life, but he always retained an interest in Canada.

Ulster contacts had been useful to Joseph McGaw in the land of his adoption, and church connections were obviously helpful to William McKinney. When some of the rest of the family went to Australia, they now had the advantage of relatives already living there. In 1861 William John McGaw went out to join his brother Joseph on the Wilson land, but in spite of this contact he found the life difficult and returned to Ireland several times. In February 1870 he married Sarah McKinney, and brought her back to Australia with him.

Their first home was at Pomingalarna where William managed the station. A letter of Sarah's, dated 20 March 1871, described a domestic scheme which was very different from the one she had left:

> Our luggage arrived in a bullock dray about a month after us. W.J. put up the sowing machine and I have been working with it. The heat has been 100° in the shade. The grapes, peaches and almonds are almost done. We were greatly robbed by the parrots and laughing jackasses. Wm John is very busy and has worked two or three stone of flesh off him.

For the menfolk, life on these remote stations was busy and exciting but it was not so for the women. In June she wrote: 'There is very little news here, one week is very like the other before it to me.'

Other relatives joined the McGaws in Australia. William McKinney's sons, Joseph and Thomas George, went out to work on the Kooba station in 1880 and were joined ten years later by the youngest member of the family, William James. The final member of the family to go to Australia was Hugh McKinney, William's brother, although he did not work on a station. After qualifying as an engineer and working for a year on Irish canals, Hugh went to India in 1869. For nine years he was involved in canal construction work in the Punjab and in 1877 was appointed Canal Magistrate of the North West Province of India. In 1879 he, his wife and their two children left India for Australia. A letter to his mother dated 12 November 1879 describes the journey and the family:

> Since we left Bombay on the 8th inst. Marian has had such a time as she never had before and hopes never to have again. Our eldest daughter is very lively and a terrible mischief so that she requires incessant watching . . . Both David

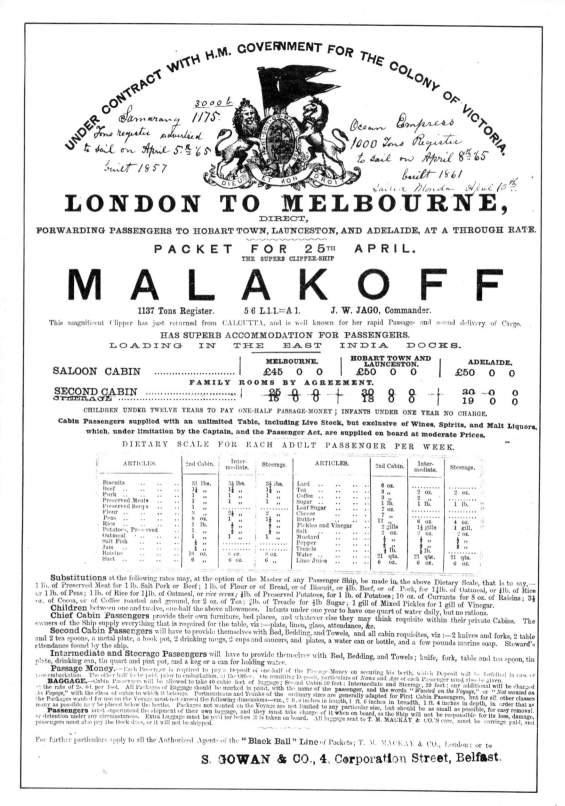

Hugh and Samuel McKinney in an informal pose at Galway where they both attended the Queen's College, 1867. Note the studio's self-promoting design on the reverse of the mount (*above*).

McMordie [his brother-in-law] and Marian say that Elsie is like you and I think there is some ground for the idea. At any rate she is like you in her tastes to some extent as she would drink any reasonable quantity of tea we would give her! . . . She is a little spoiled from being so much in the jungle where there were no other children.

In Australia, Hugh worked for the Sydney Water Supply Board. By 1884 he was in charge of water conservation throughout New South Wales and was responsible for valuable schemes of conservation and irrigation. He drew up important reports for the harnessing of the Murray and Murrumbidgee rivers which eventually helped to improve many thousands of acres of land.

Two other McKinney brothers who went abroad were John and Samuel. John McKinney had settled with his wife and family on a farm at the Sandy Knowes, a short distance from Sentry Hill, but in 1877 they decided to emigrate. Unlike the other members of the McKinney household, they joined a party leaving for a special settlement in New Zealand. Called Kati-Kati, the scheme was the brainchild of George Vesey Stewart, a landowner from Tyrone, who in the early 1870s had visited New Zealand. Having found a suitable place for a settlement, he then persuaded a number of Ulster families to emigrate to the area. The scheme prospered and in 1877 Stewart published some notes on the undertaking and proposed that a second settlement should be started.

Travel poster, 1865, from the Sentry Hill papers.

An unidentified studio portrait of John McKinney and his family before their departure for New Zealand, 1877.

The pamphlet, of which there is a copy at Sentry Hill, made it clear that the scheme was not open to everyone:

Mechanics, artisans, millworkers, hacklers, and young gentlemen with soft hands, without money, prospects or brains would exist better at home.

He looked for people from a farming background with some capital. John McKinney and his family were very suitable and they set sail from Carrickfergus on 20 May 1878 aboard the *Lady Jocelyn*. In spite of the glowing promises held out for the scheme, the new arrivals did not find everything to their liking. Problems arose over the way the land had been surveyed and a protest meeting of the emigrants in 1880 objected to the way the land had been allocated. Life seems to have been hard in the early days: William McKinney's diaries record money and clothes being sent out to John and family. Eventually John became a Presbyterian minister in the area.

Samuel McKinney attended the Queen's Colleges in Belfast and Galway and then took a medical degree at Edinburgh, qualifying in 1876. For reasons of health he served as a ship's physician on a number of voyages to

Dr Hugh McKinney lying on the grass at his home in Mornington, London, 1910 (W.McK.). *Standing:* Elsie McKinney and Miss Stevens. *Seated:* Mrs McKinney and her mother, Mrs Stevens.

warm climes during the years 1877–9. In the winter of 1878–9 he visited the Cape of Good Hope and brought home two ostrich eggs which are still at Sentry Hill. He eventually set up practice in London. Samuel was later to publish five books on religious and moral subjects, including the work on Darwin already mentioned, another volume entitled *Disease and Sin: a new textbook for medical and divinity students,* and an anthology of poetry.

The last McKinney to go abroad was William's son, Hugh Giffin McKinney. After receiving his early education in Belfast, Hugh went to live with his uncle Samuel in London and continued his medical training at St Bartholomew's Hospital. During the Boer War he served as a medical volunteer. The first letters from South Africa in early 1900 describe setting up a field hospital at Bloemfontein. He writes to his sister Maggie:

> I am chief surgical wardmaster and Jack Dunn is chief medical wardmaster. We have to supervise the men attending the patients. We have each 36 marquees with 8 beds in each.

Hugh was very critical of Chamberlain's role in the war and had a poor

200

opinion of the army doctors. He enjoyed meeting soldiers from the colonies and remarked on meeting Australians who knew some of his relatives in Australia. To begin with much of the time was spent dealing with dysentery or typhoid cases, but later wounded soldiers were brought down from the front line.

Photograph taken during Joe McKinney's visit home in 1902. *Left to right:* Meg McKinney, Tom McKinney, Joe McKinney and John McKinney.

> One of my patients is a prisoner – he belongs to the Boer Irish Brigade. His name is Dunne and he left Ireland ten years ago. I delighted him and the colonials in the ward by telling him that he would be treated just as if he were an Englishman! – that we who wore the red cross were neutrals.

By July, work at the hospital was very hectic with train-loads of wounded soldiers arriving at all times of the day and night. By October he had been withdrawn to a hospital in Pretoria and early in the following year he returned to England. He qualified as a doctor and later became a senior medical officer in Nigeria.

Thus members of the McKinney family travelled and settled far afield. Not all were as successful as Joseph McGaw but most prospered and

146

undoubtedly to a greater extent than if they had stayed at home. Early in the twentieth century some of these people and their children returned to see Sentry Hill. A number of William McKinney's photographs cover their visits. While the skills they acquired at home in Carnmoney and even the capital they sometimes brought with them benefited their adopted countries, so the gifts of money which they made to the people at home were of considerable value. Joe McGaw in the 1860s had sent money to his sister on several occasions for the education of the young McKinney children. On the death of Sarah McGaw in 1922 a considerable amount of money was left to her Irish relatives and this helped Sentry Hill through the lean period of the 1920s. Above all these international contacts made Sentry Hill part of a much wider world than would have been thought possible at the beginning of the nineteenth century.

6
Modern Times

When war broke out in the late summer of 1914, life at Sentry Hill was set in a prosperous, contented pattern and the future seemed certain. The farm extended to 76 acres of well-cultivated and drained land. William's grandson Tom had returned from agricultural college two years earlier to take over the running of the farm. He had had the byre reconstructed and plans had already been laid for further improvements. For the time being he lived at Sentry Hill with his father John, grandfather William, Aunt Meg and sister Elsie. By the end of the war, however, the picture had dramatically changed. Two members of the household were dead, the plans for modernisation were shelved, and the future of the farm and home was in serious jeopardy.

Tom McKinney enlisted late in 1914. He did not join the 36th Ulster Division as might have been expected but enlisted in the public schools' regiment, for which he was eligible because he had attended the Royal Belfast Academical Institution. At Sentry Hill there are cards and letters sent by Tom to all his family, especially sister Elsie, from his training camp in England and then from France. This correspondence reveals the countryman's interests which he carried with him. On 6 May 1915 he writes from Epsom:

> We are having fine weather here at present and the trees are becoming green. I don't think this county is any earlier than Co. Antrim and certainly not so early as Co. Down.

When he arrives in France he continues to write to his people about the countryside. The letters now carry the seal of the army censor so there is little detail about the war. News from Sentry Hill always interests him. He writes to his father on 6 January 1916, 'it is a pity you didn't get the potatoes up in the autumn' – perhaps the absence of Tom and others at the Front meant labour was hard to find at Sentry Hill. Gifts from home such as cigarettes and copies of *The Northern Whig* are gratefully acknowledged. On 16 January 1916 he thanks his Aunt Meg for her letter and gifts: 'I received the plum duff [plum pudding] and ate part of it today, cold, and found it quite good.'

In early July, however, correspondence of a different type began to arrive at Sentry Hill. The McKinneys would no doubt have read of the Somme offensive but they would not have realised that Tom was involved in it until a telegram, dated 6 July 1916, arrived from the infantry record office in Hounslow, England: 'Regret to inform you your son 5265 Pte.

WAKEFIELD, EPSOM.
Tom.   Jack McDowell

Postcard home from Tom McKinney, *fourth on left*, early 1915, from camp in England.

McKinney dangerously wounded. 23rd clearing Stn. regret permission to visit him cannot be granted.'

The shock of this message may have been somewhat alleviated by a more detailed note from a J.W. Ekin which arrived shortly afterwards.

Dear Mr McKinney   4/7/16

Your son was slightly wounded yesterday with a piece of a bomb which struck him on the hip. I can assure you that you need not have the slightest anxiety as to 'Mac's' (as he is known to everybody) condition. I don't know if he has ever mentioned my name to you but we were at Inst. together and came over to Epsom together.

An official note a few days later stated that Tom had been evacuated to base. Then from No 1 General Hospital, a letter dated 10 July arrived from him.

Dear Father,

I am sure that you have been told a few times already that I have been wounded. I am going on as well as can be expected but it will be a very slow business. I cannot write much as I am very tired and sore. Hoping all at home are quite well,
        I remain, your affectionate son, Tom.

A series of brief notes now began to arrive daily from a Sister Dempster at the General Hospital. The patient seemed to be improving until 14 July when they were informed that he was not quite so well as the previous day. By 17 July he was dangerously ill but 'he was *so pleased* to get your letter yesterday – will you write frequently to him to cheer him up?'

149

No. _104._

Regiment _20 S.B.R.F_   Army Form B. 295.

PASS.

No. _____ (Rank) _Pt:_ (Name) _McKinney TG_

has permission to be absent from his quarters, from

Dec 2. 1914 to _Dec 29th_

for the purpose of proceeding to _Belgns:_

(Station) _Epsom:_   _for HJ Bickley Capt_
                              Commanding.

(Date) _Dec 23 1914_   _Epson Det—_

Pass for Private McKinney.

THOMAS GEORGE M'KINNEY,

PRIVATE,

20TH BATTALION ROYAL FUSILIERS

(PUBLIC SCHOOLS),

WOUNDED JULY 3rd, DIED JULY 19th, 1916.

———

Mr John T. M'Kinney and Family

thank you for your kindness and sympathy

in their bereavement.

Sentry Hill,
Carnmoney.

Printed letter from the McKinneys
about the death of Tom.

Tom McKinney, on his last leave
home before going to France in
1915 (W.McK.).

Three days later the family was told of his death by Sister Dempster. An official letter a couple of days later confirmed that he had died on 19 July. The wound in his hip had become infected with gas gangrene.

Two more letters now arrived from France. The first, written on the day of Tom's death, was from a Sister Harrington in the hospital. She explained that as she had recently come from a military hospital in Belfast, he 'asked me to write and let his parents know if anything happened to him and to say he was quite happy and resigned'. He had received every attention and was 'a great favourite here'. She went on:

His wounds were very severe – the right hip being shattered and he suffered greatly from shock. I wonder how he lived so long – he must have been a very strong boy. He was always talking about his home and Belfast.

The second letter, dated 20 July, came from a Presbyterian chaplain.

I saw him the day before yesterday and he spoke of you all at home and only wished he was back again in Carnmoney, where he was sure he would get well, but of course it was impossible to move him or think of sending him to England.

I saw him again yesterday, and I think he knew the end was coming, and was resigned. I prayed with him and he knew me, but later in the aft. when I went again, he was fast losing consciousness, and really past all pain. He passed away quietly at the last.

I can only commend you to the loving care of Our Heavenly Father in your great sorrow. To me it is an honour as I had got to know him well. His last conscious thoughts were of you all.

Believe me with sincere sympathy.
Ever faithfully yours,
J. Lynn C. F.

Subsequent official communication informed the family that he had been buried at the French Souvenir cemetery, St Omer. In early 1917 his uniform and personal effects arrived back home.

Tom's death at the early age of twenty-three was a stunning blow to the family at Sentry Hill. Isobel Crozier recalls seeing William McKinney crying in the garden with his grandson's cap in his hands. All Tom's letters, cards and papers were carefully put away. His death was of course only one of numerous deaths of Carnmoney people at the war. But besides the personal loss of a much beloved son and grandson it meant the collapse of well-laid plans for Sentry Hill. All this cast an air of sorrow and gloom over old William McKinney's last months.

Despite his advanced age, William McKinney still kept up his duties as congregational secretary. The committee books for 10 April 1917, however, carried the following statement:

It may be placed on record for the information of future generations that a violent snowstorm set in on the afternoon of this day and continued most of the night. On account of the roads rapidly filling up the committee, out of tender consideration for the aged secretary, persuaded him against his will, but in a most kindly manner, to go home before the business had concluded. This was the last meeting held in his lifetime.

Sentry Hill in snow, 1914 (W.McK.).

152

On the evening of 25 April William left the drawing room to look for a book for a guest. His daughter, Meg, heard a loud cry and rushed to him but he died in her arms. He was buried beside his wife Eliza in Carnmoney cemetery.

John McKinney was now master of Sentry Hill. The next period in the history of the farm and home until John's death in 1934 was not a prosperous one. In part this was due to lack of full attention to the farm by John, undoubtedly a result of the loss of his only son. To a greater extent, however, it was a consequence of the great depression which hit all Ulster farming from the early 1920s onwards. Prices of farm produce fell drastically. Labourers and small farmers continued to leave the land and their cottages fell derelict. Land which had been worked for and purchased at high prices in the last century now commanded low prices. When John died the only McKinneys at Sentry Hill were Meg, John's sister, and his daughter Elsie, neither of whom could cope with the farm. The sale of Sentry Hill was a distinct possibility. Help, when it came, was from a quarter that William McKinney would not have expected in 1917. In 1934 Dr Joe McKinney Dundee, son of William's daughter Janet, took over the running of Sentry Hill. In 1941 Elsie McKinney signed the farm over to Joe, who maintained her and her aunt at Sentry Hill for the rest of their lives.

Funeral of Mr. W. Fee M'Kinney

The remains of the late Mr. William Fee M'Kinney were interred on Saturday in Carnmoney Burying-ground. A very large assemblage of the relatives and friends of the deceased were present to show their respect for one who for many years had occupied a deservedly high place in the community. Mr. M'Kinney, who had reached the ripe age of 84, was the possessor of a mind of very superior capabilities and decided tastes. In the midst of his duties as a farmer he found time to give a good deal of attention to literary and antiquarian subjects, and amassed a large number of rare and valuable books and curios. To matters connected with the Linen Hall Library, the Belfast Naturalists' Field Club, and the Assembly's Historical Society he gave a good deal of attention. He was a life-long member of Carnmoney Presbyterian Church, and acted as secretary with a zeal that could not be surpassed. The services in the house and at the graveside were conducted by the Revs. H. Waterworth, M.A.; Craig Houston, B.D.; and J. M'Ilwrath, B.A.

Janet McKinney had married Isaac Dundee in 1895. The Dundees had been doctors in Carnmoney for several generations and, indeed, had attended the McKinneys from the 1850s. Isaac had gone to India as a doctor for 15 years, and served in the army during the third Burmese war. In 1894 he returned to Carnmoney village where he became dispensary and family doctor as well as registrar. Isaac and Janet had five children – Jack, Bessie, Isobel, William, and Joe.

Isobel recalls today her childhood visits to her grandfather's home.

Sentry Hill . . . was a second home for us children . . . The road was uphill, the highest part overlooked the valley of the Three Mile Water which ended with a spectacular view of the Antrim hills and Slemish. It was here that Great-Grandfather, T. G. McKinney, coming from church, would stop, look at the view and say 'What a wonderful world.' We walked down the back avenue past the fairy thorn and into the yard of Sentry Hill, where friendly dogs, Old Bruin and Paddy, were ready to greet us. We would look carefully to see the swing was in position in the shed before going into the house.

Inside the kitchen the big range was warm and welcoming, often with the delicious smell of freshly baked bread. The rocking chair stood in front, and old Polly, the parrot, made clucking noises in his cage. The funny distorting mirror hanging on the wall never failed to make us laugh. We would hurry to speak to Grandfather writing at his desk in the breakfast room before greeting our Aunt.

Sundays were different from weekdays. After church everyone was hungry for the large roast beef dinner in the dining room; for the later evening meal it

was usual for twelve or more to sit round the table and very often with unexpected guests. The lamp light gave a warm soft glow very different from the harsh electric light of today. At this meal we had eggs baked in little dishes or jellied chicken, macaroni cheese, with apple cake, sponge cake, potato bread, scones, etc. We would leave Sentry Hill about seven or eight o'clock, remembering the long walk home. We groped our way up the avenue in the darkness of the overhanging trees, and were glad to emerge onto the road. I remember vividly the large expanse of sky, brilliantly lit with stars in the clean atmosphere of those days. Other memories that remain are seeing the first snowdrops in spring; they were planted in the form of a name – Sarah, a sister of Grandfather's who went to Australia. At Easter our Aunt dyed a few dozen eggs with whin blossom for us children to trundle down the garden. Thick masses of primroses and violets grew in the banks of the front avenue which we loved to gather.

In 1910 Isaac Dundee was killed in an accident when his trap overturned on the Mossley Brae. Seven years later his widow and family moved to Belfast, to be near educational facilities. Both Bessie and Jack joined up, but the war finished before they could be sent abroad: both then became doctors. Isobel, who married Dr Harold Crozier, became a leading member of the Belfast Naturalist Field Club, serving as president for a time and pursuing many of the interests of her grandfather.

The member of the family most involved with Sentry Hill, however, was the youngest, Joe. From his earliest moments he was a constant visitor at Sentry Hill. After Carnmoney National School he went on to the Royal Belfast Academical Institution, but during school time he still came out to the farm every weekend.

In 1924, following the Dundee tradition, Joe went to Queen's University to study medicine. Five years later he qualified – in spite of time off for dancing and hunting! After a period as a senior houseman in the Belfast City Hospital, and some time as a ship's doctor, Joe returned to East Antrim, to Whitehead, only eighteen miles from Carnmoney and set up in practice there in 1932. From here he visited Sentry Hill nearly every week, so he kept up both the medical and the farming sides of his family. His experience in these fields is a valuable record of the changes in the countryside from the 1920s onwards.

When Joe started up at Whitehead, his income for the first nine months amounted to the princely sum of 18s. 6d. and £3.6s.0d. in bad debts. During the next three months, however, he made £120. Thereafter the practice expanded and prospered. In 1935 he became the local dispensary doctor. As such, Joe took part in a system established in the early nineteenth century to help the less well-off, who could not afford to pay private fees. The doctor had to master all the skills of the profession, without modern-day access to the specialists. He still prepared and dispensed his own medicines. This continued until the system was abolished in 1948.

In the 1930s, when Joe first went into general practice, medicine had not altered much from his father's time. But the introduction of penicillin and

Isaac and Janet Dundee with their youngest child Joe, 1908 (W.McK.).

Joe Dundee on a donkey with his cousin Tom McKinney, 1908 (W.McK.).

other antibiotics led to tremendous changes. As Medical Officer of Health, Joe became responsible for public health during a period which saw the eradication of tuberculosis from the Ulster countryside. He was the first in East Antrim to start immunisation against diptheria, no doubt because his brother William had died of this illness at the age of three, thus giving him a special awareness of the problem.

When Joe took over the running of Sentry Hill in 1934, the buildings and land were beginning to deteriorate. As soon as he had enough money from his practice, these matters were put to right. Due to his interest in horses, however, attention on the farm now turned increasingly from dairying to breeding and training horses. Within a couple of years the outbuildings were adapted to provide more stabling for horses. There had been four full-time labourers on the farm when Joe took over, but by the late 1940s, although store cattle were still kept at Sentry Hill, there were no resident farmhands; three outside men came in to look after the horses and cattle.

As a boy, Joe had often hunted on the family pony, Polly, but his interest

Joe and Betty Dundee at Sentry Hill not long after their wedding in 1935 (J.McK.D.).

really developed in 1924 when his uncle, John McKinney, presented him with a light chestnut horse called Ginger. Joe now began to play a leading part in the East Antrim Hounds. Twice a week during the season he would leave his practice in Whitehead, hunt from noon to 3 p.m., and return in time for the afternoon surgery! Hunting at this time was rather different from today: farmers were more flexible in their attitudes to people riding over their land, and there was considerably less wire fencing about. Joe also rode Ginger to local point-to-point races. For fifty years he was the course doctor at the Lisnalinchy races.

By the 1950s, Joe was breeding and training thoroughbreds and 'chasers'. Two of his best horses were Sentry Hill and Ballyvesey. Sentry Hill was very successful, winning various races, at Punchestown and elsewhere, and becoming the top point-to-pointer in the North of Ireland. The training of horses at the farm continued until the 1960s, and many of them were raced by Joe himself.

During all this time Joe was still living at Whitehead (to be near his patients). In the summer of 1935 he met Betty Mellon on a visit back to Co. Antrim from South Africa where her parents now lived. That Christmas Joe went out to Cape Town and they were married in the Anglican Cathedral there. They returned to set up home at the Promenade, Whitehead. In 1938 he volunteered to the Medical War Committee but

John and Robin Dundee with horse on training reins at Sentry Hill, 1949 (J.McK.D).

John and Robin Dundee with dogs and pet rabbit on the front lawn of Sentry Hill, 1947 (J.McK.D.).

had to remain at his practice during the war. Two sons were born, one, John, now a successful radiologist in Missouri, the other, Robin, a farmer at Islandmagee. After fifteen years' illness, caused by malignant hypertension, Betty died in 1960.

The last two decades have seen considerable changes at Sentry Hill and the surrounding area. Elsie McKinney had already sold the Mallusk farm in the 1930s and a new motorway cut off a further 11 acres from the Sentry Hill holdings in the 1960s. Part of the Fairymount farm was now at the other side of the motorway and a large detour was necessary to reach it, so eventually Fairymount was sold. The land at Mallusk is now taken up by industrial units, while the neighbouring townlands of Glengormley and Carnmoney have been completely built up.

In 1964 Meg McKinney, who had lived at Sentry Hill all her life, died, and thirteen years later her niece, Elsie, had to leave the house for a nursing home where she died in 1979.

By 1977 Joe had retired and he moved to Sentry Hill, with all his books

and photographs. His library reflects the wide interests he has pursued all his life. Besides books on horses, hunting and nature, there are many volumes on history and archaeology. As a keen photographer he has built up a good collection of wild life and flower photographs which show well the changes in the natural history of the countryside over the last fifty years. Corncrakes and kestrels, for example, so beautifully illustrated in Joe's photographs, are now a rarity around Carnmoney, thanks to new farming methods.

Since moving to Sentry Hill, Joe has been busy working in the garden and maintaining the house and outbuildings. He and his sister Isobel have carefully sorted out their grandfather's papers and photographs. There are no longer horses at Sentry Hill and the fields are let to neighbouring farmers. But Joe looks after three rather wild dogs, and the occasional badger and fox, as well as the bird life around the house. No less than his grandfather, Joe continues to pursue his 'great curiosity' about the world around him and Sentry Hill remains a very special place to visit. Where the future now lies for Sentry Hill is not certain but it is hoped that this book will serve as a record of the house and the remarkable family which has lived there for so long.

Joe Dundee with Sentry Hill after a win at the Lisnalinchy races, 1956.

Acknowledgements

My thanks are due to the many people who have helped in the writing of this book. Mr Wesley McCann rendered invaluable assistance by sorting out and cataloguing the books at Sentry Hill. At an early stage of the work the Arts Council of Northern Ireland gave me a generous research grant for which I am extremely grateful. Transcripts of some of the diaries, made by Mr Brian Trainor of the Public Record Office of Northern Ireland, were very helpful. For their assistance with the photographic material I wish to thank Mr Dermott Dunbar, Mr Herbert Carlisle, Mr Mervyn Jones and the members of the photographic units at the Ulster Folk Museum and Queen's University. Acknowledgement is paid to the Public Record Office of Northern Ireland and the Royal Irish Academy for permission to reprint material from the Ordnance Survey Memoirs. Finally, I must thank all the members of the Dundee family for their help. The sorting of material by Mrs Isobel Crozier and her notes on the family history greatly assisted my work. To Dr Joe Dundee I am extremely grateful for allowing me to see and use the Sentry Hill material.

Afternoon tea at Sentry Hill, *c.*1900
(W.McK.). *Left to right:* an
unidentified friend, Tom
McKinney, Elsie McKinney and
Meg McKinney.

1869

Sun 18th July. Went to Carnmoney & heard Mr Barkley preach. Sam recd a private registered letter from Hugh £11/—

Mon 19th I pulled the remainder of the thistles and the docans and while daisies out of the low field corn and carried them off! Sam got the new scythe hung at Billey Patricks. and commenced to mow the meadow

Tues 20th Sam mowed. Hannah tead I assisted after noon

Wed 21. Sam mowed. I assisted Hannah to lead and coil. churned Sarah drined the butter.

Thurs 22 Wrote and posted a letter to Hugh. went to town with milk and butter. posted two papers to Mr Stewart Sam got done mowing the meadow Hannah tead

Fri 23d Sam Hannah and I tead and coiled in the meadow. there came on a shower after dinner. pulled thistles and other weeds in the fore field

Sat 24. S & H turned at the hay until dinnertime when there came on rain coiled about an hour. pulled thistles up at the pitsteads

Sun 25. Went to Carnmoney and heard Mr Smyth of Whitehouse preach

Hannah became unwell and came home

Mon 26. Turned and coiled hay in the meadow got my boot mended at R Carlisles there were some showers

Tues 27th July. Sam Hannah & I built six ricks in the meadow after dinner H & I coiled until 12 o'c

Wed 28. S. H. & I built five ricks there came on rain after dinner with a great deal of thunder next Belfast Churner. Scalded wasps in three nests

Thurs 29. Went to town with milk and butter. Sam drove manure from the byre to the meadow. this was a very wet day after eleven o'c

Fri 30 Scaled manure in the meadow until 10 o'c after brought seven of the ricks from the mid park to the stackyard

Sat 31. Brought the remaening two ricks from the mid park and finished the pike in the back garden with it. Sam shore grass up the loanin. Hannah and I scaled manure in the meadow

Sun 1st August went to Carnmoney and heard Mr Woods a young minister preach My Father & Mother rec. a letter from Hugh

Mon 2d. Wrought in the meadow put up five ricks

Tues 3d A wet day. I wrote to Hugh

Wed 4. Sam & I drove John's flax from our W. hill to my fathers bog. churned

Thurs 5. Went to town with milk and butter. put up the last three ricks in the meadow after I came home posted letters to Joseph and Hugh & a paper to W.S.

A sample opening from William McKinney's diary for the year 1869. It was written into an old account book.

Sources

The main source for this book has been the collection of manuscript and contemporary printed papers at Sentry Hill. The diaries of William McKinney have been photocopied and can be seen at the Public Record Office of Northern Ireland (Ref. no. T.3234). All documents referred to in the text have also been copied and these will be placed in the P.R.O.N.I. after publication of this book. For developments in the Carnmoney area prior to the nineteenth century an invaluable source has been H.J. St J. Clarke's *Thirty Centuries in South-East Antrim* (Belfast, 1938). Nathan Todd's unpublished M.A. thesis, 'A social and economic study of part of South County Antrim in the second half of the nineteenth century,' proved an extremely important guide to agricultural developments in Co. Antrim. The minute books for the Carnmoney Presbyterian church committee and session are to be found in the library of the Presbyterian Historical Society in Belfast and in Carnmoney church. The extracts from the Ordnance Survey Memoirs have come from the transcripts of these memoirs in the P.R.O.N.I.; the original papers are in the Royal Irish Academy in Dublin.